ÛPTIME

ÛPTIME

A Practical Guide to Personal
Productivity and Wellbeing

LAURA MAE MARTIN

GOOGLE'S PRODUCTIVITY EXPERT

HARPER
BUSINESS

An Imprint of HarperCollinsPublishers

HarperCollins books may be purchased for educational, business, or sales promotional use. For information, please email the Special Markets Department at SPsales@harpercollins .com.

FIRST EDITION

Designed by Nancy Singer

Illustrations by Ma'ayan Rosenzweig

Library of Congress Cataloging-in-Publication Data

Names: Martin, Laura Mae, author.
Title: Uptime : a practical guide to personal productivity and wellbeing /
    Laura Mae Martin.
Identifiers: LCCN 2023045469 (print) | LCCN 2023045470 (ebook) | ISBN
    9780063317444 (hardcover) | ISBN 9780063317468 (ebook)
Subjects: LCSH: Time management. | Work-life balance.
Classification: LCC HD69.T54 M3823 2024 (print) | LCC HD69.T54 (ebook) |
    DDC 650.1/1—dc23/eng/20231006

LC record available at https://lccn.loc.gov/2023045469
LC ebook record available at https://lccn.loc.gov/2023045470

24 25 26 27 28 LBC 5 4 3 2 1

For my Weekly Tippers,

And for Jake, the best thing that ever happened to me was you ☺

CONTENTS

PART IV   HOW TO DO IT WELL

PART V   HOW TO LIVE WELL WHILE DOING IT ALL

UPTIME

I spent last Saturday binge-watching old episodes of *Heartland* in a nonstop, ten-hour marathon while snacking on popcorn, broken up only by one half-hour catnap in the early afternoon.

And that day was one of the most productive days of my life.

How could that be?

According to the rules of the "old productivity," working hard, working more, and working all the time are the keys to getting things done. Why "waste" a Saturday when you could be checking things off your list? Too often productivity has been defined as *how much* we check off our list. But how do we know that the things on our list are the right things? How do we know that the time slot in which we've chosen to do something is going to produce the best output based on our energy levels? If we did too many things today, are we going to be too burnt-out to generate good ideas tomorrow?

When your intention matches your action, it's productive. In the above example, my husband kindly volunteered to take my three kids to his parents' for the day so I could have a break. My *intention* was to relax and finish watching one of my favorite series. My *action* was to comfortably enjoy it all from the couch without interruption. The combination of those two made it a productive day.

Productivity is 1) Defining clearly what you want to do, 2) Setting aside the (right) time and place to do it, and 3) Executing well within the designated time. The consistent practice of these three things we can define as finding your *Uptime*.

Uptime in the computer world is the time that a computer is operational and productive. In your world, Uptime is the time that you're operational and productive, no matter what you're choosing to do. Your Uptime may be a job but it also may be parenting, owning your own business, being a student or even an artist. Uptime does not just refer to your peak productivity hours, but rather, all of the energy that flows through you during your most productive day. Uptime is when you're feeling "in the zone," getting things done, checking items off your to-do list. It's also when you're relaxed and present during the time you've chosen to detach and unwind. It's feeling great while doing whatever it is you've intended to do.

I like to think of finding your Uptime as synonymous with "flow." It's when you're setting intentions and easily following through on them because you've created an environment that allows you to thrive. It's more than just getting things done. It's the energy that comes with having clarity and focus, the ease you feel as you navigate your day and your week. It's feeling your best and producing results—both at work and in your personal life. Uptime means feeling productive *and* energized.

Let's throw away the idea that productivity is busy, back-to-back, or being constantly "on." Instead, let's replace this outdated version of productivity with the idea of *Uptime*. Out with chaos and in with calm. Out with busy and in with balance. Out with our old ideas of productivity and in with the new state of Uptime.

Uptime starts with a grounded understanding of yourself as a whole person. What makes you happy at work and outside of work? What are your natural rhythms and peak times for creativity, focus, or efficiency? When are you most engaged in meetings? What makes you feel unstoppable when responding to emails? When do you need to take a break, do some uninterrupted thinking, or deepen social connections?

Uptime ~~takes a h~~olistic view—what we can accomplish, how we accomplish it, how happy we are, and how that contributes to things like innovation, job retention, and burnout. The pandemic years showed us that the "butts in seats from nine to five" model is no longer the most viable one. We now need the tools and skills to manage our workloads, our time, and our own schedules to be better workers and happier people.

Uptime is operating at a level that's sustainable. The difference between a busy day and a productive day comes down to energy, attention, and impact. It's about leveraging time and focus. It's not the tools, but the *intention* behind the tools, that matters most.

Uptime doesn't happen by mistake, it happens by design. It's a matter of carefully curated priorities and excellence in execution. It follows a set of principles that I've refined over more than ten years of coaching executives and developing training for my colleagues at Google.

And now I'm bringing Uptime to you.

WHY ME?

I began at Google almost fourteen years ago in a sales role. Managing over fifty client relationships, at first I found myself overwhelmed by the number of requests coming in. So I organized my inbox in a way that made it a workflow dashboard. I started scheduling my sales calls Tuesday through Thursday only, so I could prepare on Monday and send client wrap-up notes on Friday. People were wondering how I was always on top of my work and keeping my clients (and myself) happy. Colleagues started asking me about how I organized myself to maintain this output. How was I hitting my targets without being the first one in the office each day, or the last one to leave? It soon became clear that sales wasn't my sweet spot; managing my time and workflow was.

Over the next eight years I developed the Productivity@Google program and started working with all Googlers, from Nooglers (new Googlers) to executives. I developed training sessions to teach others throughout the company my methods for productivity. I now work in the Office of the CEO, where I coach and train executives on strategies for getting more done, and how to remain calm and grounded while doing it. I've used Google Workspace tools—from Gmail to Meet—to help interns, new employees, midlevel engineers, our most senior executives, and employees of every level at other companies to master productivity. I started publishing a newsletter that a third of all Google employees have subscribed to, and my workshops have been taken and highly rated by tens of thousands of professionals. And I've done it all while building a family—with three kids under the age of four!

This book isn't a book just for Googlers. And it's not a book just for executives or even just for workers. It's a book for *anyone* who wants to be the owner of their time, anyone who wants to ride that feeling of calm accomplishment. It's a guide for employees, students, parents, and entrepreneurs alike.

I wrote this book to bring everything I've learned about productivity to you. By the end of this book you'll feel lighter, more excited, and more in control of the things you need to get done—at work and in your personal life. Perhaps more importantly, you'll feel permission to *not* do something when you know it's *not* the right time—so when it *is* the right time, you'll execute with excellence.

The book is broken down into five parts:

1. *What* to do: How to choose your priorities and how to say no to all the rest
2. *When* to do it: How to learn and capitalize on your natural productivity peaks and valleys
3. *Where* to do it: How to take advantage of the environments where you work, whether you're hybrid, always at home, or always at a workplace
4. *How* to do it well: How to execute on the things you've decided to do with absolute excellence and efficiency

5. How to live well *while* doing it: How to be happy, successful, and
   mindful while getting it all done

I'll start by introducing the principles of productivity that you'll see
mentioned throughout the chapters. Many of my teachings are grounded
in these ideas and we'll continue to reference them through the book.

THE PRINCIPLES OF PRODUCTIVITY

Productivity = Vision + Execution

Ever since the industrial revolution, with its emphasis on output per
worker and assembly line metrics, we've focused on productivity as a
practice of efficiency and output. However, the most productive individuals actually have both of these important attributes: vision *and* execution.
Let's think of a "loop" as anything pending that's floating around in your
brain—an idea, something you need to buy, something you "thought of,"
an insight, a next step, something you need to tell someone. Opening
more new loops is *vision*—ideas coming together, letting things soak in,
thinking about two items in a related sense where you haven't before (the
definition of creativity), or coming up with something you should do or
a new way to solve a problem. Closing those loops is *execution*—crossing
those things off a to-do list, taking next steps, and acting on your vision.
Someone with good vision opens a lot of loops. Someone with good execution closes them. A productive person does both: they have the vision,
then they execute on it.

Opening a loop is having a great idea on your daily run about how
to solve an issue for your team. Closing the loop is sending an email to
your team about how to act on that idea. Your day is spent in the cycle of
closing and opening loops. Many people get so bogged down in closing
loops that they don't make time for the new loops to present themselves.
They *execute* but they don't *envision*. Others have lots of great ideas,

but never put them into action. You need both. If you're closing loops, or crossing things off your to-do list, but you're not also generating new ideas, brainstorming, thinking long term, or coming up with creative solutions (opening new loops), then you're only hitting half of the productivity equation.

When I ask executives where they think of their best ideas (or "new loops"), their top three answers are 1) *the shower*, 2) *my commute*, 3) *doing something restful and unrelated* (like cooking or walking my dog). Our brains need these downtimes to recuperate and spark new ideas. Conversely, their answers never include when they're knee-deep in meetings or when they're triaging their inbox. There's less space in those activities for new loops to surface.

5 C's of Productivity

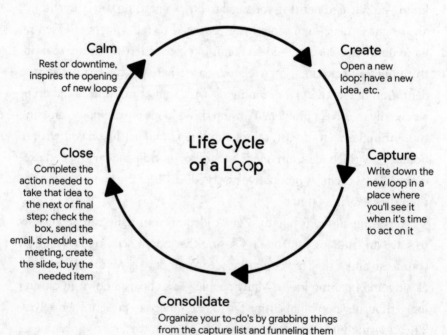

Calm
Rest or downtime, inspires the opening of new loops

Create
Open a new loop: have a new idea, etc.

Life Cycle of a Loop

Close
Complete the action needed to take that idea to the next or final step; check the box, send the email, schedule the meeting, create the slide, buy the needed item

Capture
Write down the new loop in a place where you'll see it when it's time to act on it

Consolidate
Organize your to-do's by grabbing things from the capture list and funneling them into actions for each week and day

Like a rubber band, you must pull back and stop before launching at full potential. Rest time *is* productive time if you're strategic about it.

Understanding the full life cycle of a loop helps us understand the value of vision and execution.

In its life cycle, a loop moves through what I call the *5 C's of Productivity*. We'll touch on each of these stages in the chapters to come: how to find *calm* moments that *create* new ideas, how and where to *capture* new ideas, and most importantly, how to have a process that *consolidates* all of those loops into an easy-to-follow system that makes sure you finish each loop or *close* it.

Let's look at an example of the *5 C's of Productivity* by following a loop through its life cycle:

- *Calm:* You've made time to go on a walk after work with your dog
- *Create:* An idea comes to you that would be great to present to one of your sales clients for their upcoming campaign
- *Capture:* You make a note of that in your phone and later, transfer it into your List Funnel (more on lists and this process in Chapter 3)
- *Consolidate:* That evening you make your list for the following day and schedule time to call your client about the idea at 10:00 a.m.
- *Close:* You speak to your client and implement the addition to their campaign

This is the constant cycle that carries you from new ideas (vision) all the way to making sure they get done (execution). Each chapter will show you how to fulfill both parts of the productivity equation.

Balance Is the New Busy

When handheld personal devices entered our lives, they gave us the idea we could save time by having everything accessible from anywhere.

But suddenly, because email was just a tap away it felt more urgent.

Meanwhile, chats and texts followed us everywhere, intruding on the present moment. The irony is that devices can end up wasting more time than they're saving, unless we're really intentional in how we use them.

Many of us also have more meetings than ever. And meetings about those meetings. Think of how many times you've asked someone about their day—or been asked about yours—only to reply with a mention of your *slammed schedule, back-to-back meetings*, and lack of time for lunch or even a bathroom break. That's old productivity talking.

We've gone too far in glorifying this working style. We've made it cool to be too busy. We've confused busy with important. Hearing it from others makes us think of them as important, but it's no way to create a sustainable working environment. Some of the highest-ranking executives have some of the loosest schedules and spend significant amounts of time brainstorming, reading industry news, creating, or just thinking alone. They see the value of unstructured time between meetings to re-group and process information. They know that simply pondering alone about problems might be their best contribution to move things forward.

So why do we perpetuate this idea that being busy is a sign of achievement? Or that attending too many meetings is a badge of honor?

Instead, I argue that *balance is the new busy*.

Treat Your Time Like a Bank Account of Energy

We all know that time is one of our most finite resources, but why do we so often act like it's limitless? You should ask yourself: Taking on a new project—what am I taking time from? New direct report—who or what will get less of my time as a result? New biweekly meeting—what would I have been doing instead during that time? If we maintain this trade-off mindset we can set priorities and find a healthy balance for ourselves at every turn. It's okay to have boundaries. In fact, it's essential. And it's okay to be very picky about what you spend your time on. You can still build social capital and be a good colleague.

We need to think about time more like a bank account. If someone asked for money from your bank account, you wouldn't say, *"Sure! Here is my routing and account number—grab however much you'd like!"* So why do we do that with our time? If someone asks for a meeting, how many of us have said, *"Sure! Grab time on my calendar!"* That's a surefire way to run down your bank balance of time. Just like you'd have a certain amount of money to spend in a daily budget, you can think of your day as having a certain amount of "energy points" that you can spend. You decide where to spend the energy points, where to gain them, and where to waste them. Certain things use or require more energy points from you and you can implement strategies to conserve energy points or use them more wisely. This book will show you several strategies for saying *no* in a friendly way to things that seem worthy but drain your time resources and energy points.

Flow + Focus = Time Better Spent

Time management is a buzzword—we want more time, we need extra time, we run out of time. But so often, even when we do find the time . . . things happen. You block your calendar from 9:00 a.m. to 11:00 a.m. Tuesday morning to work on that really important project. You open your computer, see a new email, and suddenly it's 9:13. You open the document you want to work on and spend a few minutes naming it before you get an instant message. It's 9:32 and you come back to the screen, where you notice an open tab with something you've been meaning to finish and that's easier to work on. Soon it's 10:05 and you see another email out of the corner of your eye that looks urgent, and you engage. At 10:36 you're wondering, *Is it even worth it to start this now when I only have twenty minutes before my next meeting?* Suddenly we see that time was the least of our problems.

Why does this happen?

Because time management is only the first step. It's the guardrails for being productive. But the essential ingredients are our energy flows and our focus *at* that time. Similarly, if we made the "time" during a part of the day or week where we have low energy, that time wasn't as valuable.

Not all time slots are equal. Asking me to create something new at 10:00–10:30 a.m. will look a whole lot more impressive than work I've churned out at 4:00–4:30 p.m., even though they are both thirty-minute time slots. They are not equal! My energy points are worth more in the morning than they are in the afternoon. Spending energy points at the *right* time gives you a better ROI on that energy spent by producing better results for those points. Knowing those patterns about yourself helps channel your energy to get the most done when you're scheduling this time.

Focus is equally important. How do we start off with such good intentions, and two hours of time, but get so derailed that we never dive into focused work? In later chapters, we'll discuss extensive strategies for getting *ahead* of distractions before they happen, training your brain to drop into flow and focus mode, knowing your common pitfalls, and creating an environment where distraction-free, focused work is the norm.

Don't Plan for You, Plan for *Future You*

Psychology tells us that we all have a disconnect with our current selves and our future selves. The results of a study published in the journal *Social Psychological and Personality Science* show that "people who perceived greater similarity to their future self, experienced greater life satisfaction ten years later." The same holds true for the much nearer Future You. When we try on clothes at the store, why do we sometimes think, *I don't love it but I could maybe see myself wearing it later?* Won't we be the same person later who also won't want to wear it? When we're asked ahead of time to schedule a meeting on Monday at 8:00 a.m. the day we're returning from a two-week vacation, we think *Sure!* and add it to our calendars, but we don't envision future 7:45 a.m.-Us that day trying to make that happen.

With this in mind, we want to be constantly planning for our future selves instead of our current selves. If we ask ourselves, *What will Future Me wish I had done right now?*, we find our schedules smoother, our priorities crisper, our output more effective. I challenge executives to ask, *What will Future You wish you had scheduled or not scheduled after that four-hour meeting block next week? What will End-of-Year You wish that you had spent more time on? Less time on? What will Parent-with-Grown-up-Kids You say that you wished you prioritized more during these early years?* This book will go through ways of using this mindset for anything from priority setting to hiring to meeting and calendar maintenance.

WHAT I'VE OUTLINED HERE MIGHT seem radically different from your current way of doing things. But trust me: I wouldn't have written this book if I hadn't seen these principles—and the methods I've developed with them—work countless times to help workers and executives at all levels achieve *Uptime*, a sort of productivity Zen. You'll feel completely on top of everything you have to do and have a holistic approach to thriving while doing it. By the end of this book you'll know exactly *what* you should focus on, *when* the best time is to do it, *where* to do it based on your schedule, *how* to do it excellently, and how to live well *while* you're doing it all!

My promise to you is that for every minute you spend reading this book, you'll gain *at least* that much back in time savings after implementing the practices that I'll share.

The simple steps outlined in the book will enable you to capitalize on the advantages of a digital world to accomplish more while living a happy and balanced life.

Here's to achieving your *Uptime*!

PART I

What to Do

TOP THREE PRIORITIES

If I stopped you on the street and asked *What are your top three priorities right now?*, what would you say? This is the very first question I ask anyone I'm coaching. Now I'm asking you.

As I mentioned in the introduction, the first step for productivity is defining clearly what you want or need to do. I don't often refer to *goals* because they feel like far-off, long-range, "hopefully someday" activities. Instead I use *priorities* because it indicates present intention, focus, and fluidity.

Why three priorities? A 2018 study at Ohio University confirmed the long and widely held "Rule of Three" (the idea that people will remember things if they're grouped in threes) by showing that in learning, our brains seek patterns and group things together. You'll likely have more than three responsibilities or priorities in your life at any given time, but figuring out your "top three" helps drive your focus. One of the most productive people I've ever worked with is Robert Kyncl, CEO of Warner Music Group. He had his three priorities sharply defined and communicated to anyone he worked with. He had a list of tasks related to each priority and seamlessly shared them with his chief of staff, assistant, and organization. These priorities became the theme of his work and his days, which helped him focus on the right things and share a defined vision with his team. The act of defining those priorities made everything and everyone run smoother.

If I ask about your top three priorities, you, too, should be able to rattle off the answer quickly because you've already thought it through. You can reevaluate these priorities as often as weekly, but typically monthly or quarterly is more appropriate. Other priorities and activities that aren't your top three will fall into place. But if you want to fill a jar with rocks, pebbles, and sand, you have to put the biggest rocks in first. Trying to put the rocks in the jar when it is already full of pebbles and sand (less important, lower-priority things) will cause the jar to overflow even though there is unused space.

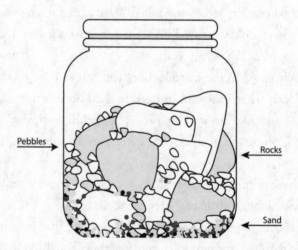

You may wonder whether I'm asking for your personal priorities or work priorities. As far as I know, you are only one person, whether you're at work or you're at home. There is just one pie of time, and one brain managing it all. Your success and fulfillment will be driven by different personal or work priorities at different times. They will swing back and forth based on your current situation and stages of life. If you're preparing to move your family across the country, this should become one of your top three priorities, bumping something else off your top three list. If you're taking on a huge project at work, something outside of work might take a backseat for a bit. It's important to narrow your top priorities down to three because it reminds you that you have to put something down to pick another thing up—there is always a trade-off.

Just as you should be able to rattle off these top priorities in a conversation, it's great to ask this of others, too. Anytime I'm working with someone new or reporting to a new leader I ask, *What are your top three priorities right now?* Just asking can help build productive and collaborative relationships by giving you a taste of what's behind the scenes and what someone is really focused on. The answer to this one simple question can give you an understanding of decisions someone is making and how they're spending their time. At one particularly overwhelming time in my life, my husband used my own tactics on me and asked, *What are your top three priorities right now?* As I started to list them off I realized I had six. No wonder I was feeling overwhelmed! Just from that one question, I realized that I was trying to focus on too many things at once. I needed to drop, delegate, or delay some things for later—and I did!

PRIORITIES ←→ TASKS

One executive I was working with defined his top three priorities for one quarter as:

1. Completing a large reorganization of his team
2. Spending more time with his young kids
3. Defining a next-year vision for the organization he was leading

Reading those overarching priorities, you may feel that they look and feel vague. The first step is defining, but you also need to figure out how to *implement* these priorities. High-impact tasks are the tangible actions that align with your priorities. Ask yourself, what high-impact tasks are involved in achieving my priorities? More specifically, how do these tasks show up on my calendar? How will I be able to recognize them? The process of working through specific *tasks* related to your priorities helps you recognize how meetings, emails, workouts, to-do's, work blocks, school events, and other things that take up time directly relate to your priorities when they come across your desk.

For each of your priorities, write down two or three high-impact tasks that support that priority (the tasks should start with an action verb):

1. **Reorganize my team**
   - Meet with my HR rep to discuss new org chart options and open positions
   - Schedule skip-level meetings to understand roles and responsibilities
   - Conduct interviews for new and open roles
2. **Spend more time with my kids**
   - Leave work by five to make family dinner three to four times a week
   - Work from home on Fridays so I can do school drop-off
   - Attend three school events during business hours this quarter (for example, concerts or conferences)
3. **Come up with my next year's team vision**
   - Prioritize unplugged/unscheduled "think time," walks, brainstorming
   - Host an all-day off-site with my direct reports to gather feedback

Defining the high-impact tasks that support your top priorities is crucial. It helps with not only what you should be focusing on generally, but also how you should be spending your time and energy points to support those priorities. It also provides a great opportunity for discussing priorities with key people in your work and life—managers, teammates, partners, spouses, and others. It provides an opportunity to confirm your priorities or adjust them based on their individual priorities and your shared goals and responsibilities. If you're working with a coworker on a huge project and it's one of your top three priorities for the quarter, but not one of theirs, that's important for you to know up front. You may need to pull in other resources or find additional help if three other huge things come before this project for your colleague. Taking the time to define priorities and get feedback on them makes later conversations about *What have you been spending your time on?* easier to navigate.

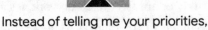

Instead of telling me your priorities,
just show me your calendar.

HOW ARE YOU TRACKING NOW?

After I ask an executive I'm coaching what their top three priorities are, I pull out their printed calendar from the last few weeks. I give them a highlighter and ask them to circle every meeting, task, or individual work time that relates to those three priorities. It quickly starts to become clear whether or not time spent is lining up with priorities. This activity is a great way to just look and see simply: *How highlighted is your calendar?* Now that you've defined what's important, are you spending *most* of your time on these things? Your time is your greatest form of currency—what you're spending time on *is* what you're prioritizing. The calendar is the truth teller. It fact-checks whether you're actually spending your time on the things that matter.

What about those things that don't fit into your top three priorities (the pebbles and sand that still need a place in the jar)? Of course you're going to be working on more than three things at any one time. Where many people go wrong is in letting those things take up most of their time and filling up all the space in the jar before they're able to get the big rocks in. Endless side projects creep up and accumulate and ultimately devour huge chunks of time. You want to reorganize your team, for example, but you're spending time in a multiday off-site meeting for a side committee. You want to spend more time with your kids but you keep doing favors or tasks outside your job that keep you from being able to leave work on time. Any of this sound familiar?

When it comes to clarifying priorities, I find it useful to think about *Future You*—the version of you that will exist weeks or months or years from now, when today's actions are in the past. What will Future You be glad that you spent time on? What will Future You be glad that you turned down so you could be more focused on the right things? If you do some type of quarterly or annual review at work, it's a good idea to write the draft at the *beginning* of the quarter to make sure you're following it closely.

One of the greatest leaders I've worked with did a yearly pre-postmortem. He did the year in review, but at the *beginning* of the year, with slides and a full presentation about how we hit our sales numbers, where we hit pitfalls and wasted some time, where we really excelled and why, and what we could have done better. Even though it was all speculation, it put us exactly in that place a year from now where *Future Us* as a team would be sitting. We even visualized how we would feel if his predictions were correct (and how we would feel if they weren't). This strategy paved the way for a successful year and got the team thinking in that "end-of-year Future-Us" mindset, before it even happened.

WHEN URGENT STRIKES . . . AGAIN

"Hi, I'm out of office today on vacation. If this is urgent, call 9-1-1.—Chad."

Chad's out-of-office message may be a bit on the snarky side, but I think we all know what he means. Things people define as "urgent" have a way of showing up regularly as "emergencies" and completely eclipsing the work they had planned.

When I'm working with someone on setting their priorities, they usually say, *"Well, this is great, and I've set my priorities, and set my time around it, and then . . . urgent things always come up!"* Depending on your role, unexpected issues requiring your immediate attention can certainly arise, making it hard to keep space in your calendar for priorities. But the best time to handle urgent matters is *before* they happen. This may seem impossible, but it only feels that way if you haven't allocated time for the urgent and unpredictable in your schedule. Here are some strategies for dealing with the urgent ahead of time:

1. **Set an urgent time block every day**

   Thomas Kurian, CEO of Google Cloud, sets an hour each day for urgent matters. He outlines this in his "How to Work with Me" guide (more on this later) and sets it for the same time every day. This way, if urgent things come up, there is always time to fit them in without affecting the rest of his calendar. Also, his team knows that this block of time is the same every day so anyone who needs to urgently speak with him can plan their time accordingly. If nothing urgent comes up, this becomes his work time or a chance to check email. This is similar to office hours held by college professors. It's always available and always at the same time, but if no one comes to chat, it becomes work time.

   Another Google executive takes a similar approach, but with a twist. She keeps a time slot free every day *without* letting her team in on the specific time. That way, if something comes up she can still make room for it if needed but she leaves it free for herself to quietly get things done if nothing urgent surfaces.

   In both examples, executives found ways to confine unexpected or urgent matters to specific spots in their schedules so the rest of their time remained unaffected.

2. **Urgent vs. important**

   One of my favorite ways for dealing with urgent matters is setting some concrete language around it. Urgent can be synonymous with many things: critical, timely, important, high profile, the list goes on. But not all urgencies are the same. So how do you triage urgent matters when they arise?

   The best way I've seen this outlined is the "Eisenhower method," based on President Dwight D. Eisenhower's 1954 remark that *"I have two kinds of problems, the urgent and the important. The urgent are not important, and the important are never urgent."* While we know things can occasionally be both, he raises a good point about identifying them. The method that has evolved from this remark defines urgent and important as follows:

Urgent: activities demanding immediate attention, usually associated with achieving someone else's goals

Important: activities that have an outcome that leads to us focusing on our priorities

URGENT VS. IMPORTANT

	URGENT	NOT URGENT
IMPORTANT	1. DO IT NOW Feel okay about completely rearranging your schedule	2. PUSH TO LATER Schedule the right time to do it, then proceed normally with current schedule
NOT IMPORTANT	3. DELEGATE QUICKLY Set a timer for "dealing" with it, minimal amount, delegate to others	4. JUST SAY NO Feel good about spending no time on these or delegate to others

Unlike Eisenhower's quote, my grid above allows for activities that are simultaneously urgent *and* important. If an item is urgent and important (Quadrant 1) you should feel comfortable dealing with it. It's worth rescheduling some meetings and/or work time because it's both time sensitive *and* aligned with your priorities. If something comes up that is important, but doesn't require immediate attention

(Quadrant 2), decide when you're going to do it and move on. If something comes up that is urgent, but not important (Quadrant 3), finding ways to deal with it that point to other resources besides *your* time can be helpful. *I understand you're locked out of your account and need to get in to work. We have a great tech desk resource that can help you with that and here is the number!* Things that are neither urgent nor important (Quadrant 4) should be things that you're comfortable spending no time on. Having your top priorities already defined makes it less tempting to spend time on things in Quadrants 3 and 4.

This can be helpful especially when you're working within a team and need to align as a group about how to deal with urgent matters when they arrive. Map problems that come up into a quadrant and decide how to deal with them as a group. In the same way that naming your feelings in a heated moment can help you identify a feeling versus just feeling "overwhelmed," mapping unexpected problems or crises on this map can help you figure out exactly how to tackle those tasks in a way that's in line with your priorities.

3. Fix the system

Urgent once, take care of it.
Urgent seventeen times . . . something is
wrong with the system.

What if you're experiencing frequent situations that fall into the first quadrant? That typically means something is broken within the system. If something urgent is coming up every single day that wasn't planned for, or wasn't thought through ahead of time, it creates an exhausting situation. It might be time to ask: *Why does this keep happening?* What systems can I put in place to avoid these things? If there are constant fire drills, how could those possibly be prevented and what changes do we need to make to workflow, communication, and processes to stop these things in their tracks? This could be a matter of designating a team or person who deals only with urgent matters. Perhaps it could require a deep dive into the last ten fire drills, to figure out what caused them to happen, and what could have been in place to prevent them.

4. **Make "dealing with urgent matters" a top three priority**

Even with all of that said and done, sometimes urgent matters are just part of the deal. Especially with certain types of roles, like journalists on deadlines or emergency room doctors, you just can't get ahead of it. Knowing that these situations will arise continually and that you'll need to make room for them when they happen is powerful because it allows you to get ahead of your schedule. This is different from having a daily urgent block because if you have a role where urgent happens often, it's not always going to seamlessly fit into the time you've allotted. You have to be more flexible to deal with the urgent matters as they come up. If you've already set time aside because you know crises will happen, the dust simply settles faster once they happen because you've made room for them mentally, and in your schedule. To make sure you have time for the unexpected, add "urgent matters" to your top three priorities list. This could look like *I'd love to lead a training for your group but given the nature of my job I leave room in my schedule every day for urgent matters so I can't commit to speaking!* In this situation you're preemptively making room for the urgent, which is right if it makes sense for your role. Emergency room doctors don't *also* have regularly scheduled patients throughout their day. They mostly leave their schedule free for urgent patients who walk in.

Now that you've defined your priorities, and made plans ahead of time for the urgent, you want to live and breathe them. They become the lens through which you view every opportunity. Write your three priorities down on a Post-it note that you place prominently on your desk to remind you. Anytime you get an email asking you to take on something new, ask yourself whether it fits onto one of the priorities on your list. If not, does it truly make sense to do it? If something comes up that isn't part of your top priorities, but you still feel it's important, then you can accept it with intention and confidence, knowing you evaluated its relevance and requirements fully, not on a whim. Maybe you'll need to think about shifting your other priorities if it's an especially demanding initiative. For example, if you become a new manager you'll have to think about how you integrate mentoring, leading, and supporting your team with your tasks as an individual contributor. It's through this type of trade-off lens that you create laser focus on exactly the right things.

So, now you've established your priorities clearly. You've identified the key tasks and actions necessary for realizing them. You've even developed strategies for dealing with the urgent issues and events that seem to blow up your calendar every day. You're in a prime position for Uptime!

But even if you're successfully sidestepping the urgent stuff, lots of things come up that want a little bit of your time. In the next chapter we'll talk about how to say no and keep those things from getting in the way of your productivity.

PRODUCTIVITY PRACTICES

- What are your top three priorities right now? What are two to three tasks or meetings that move those priorities forward?
- Print your calendar from the last two weeks and circle things that fall into those priorities. Are you comfortable with the percentage of time you're spending on them?
- Set a daily time for urgent things that come up or make it one of your top priorities and use the Urgent/Important matrix by yourself or with a team to map problems when they arise.

Chapter

2

HOW TO SAY NO

You've decided the things you want to focus on. You've identified the high-impact tasks associated with each of those priorities, and you've allocated time on your calendar for each. You've gotten buy-in from your manager/team/spouse/partner on these priorities. You're ready to go!

The difficult part is making and keeping room for these priorities in your schedule. For example, maybe you did the calendar highlight exercise from Chapter 1 and found that you're spending less than 30 percent of your time on your main priorities. (In a perfect world, it should be more like 70+ percent.) How do you clear out the rest of the clutter? How do you make sure your calendar stays true to your priorities? How do you say no to future things that may start to crowd out your priorities?

PRIORITIZING IS NOT REORDERING

When most people have a huge list of things to do, they think of prioritizing as putting the items or tasks in a specific order to figure out a way to get them all done, starting with the most important and finishing with the least. In Uptime, you should now think of prioritizing as figuring out

Say no to everything, except
the things you say yes to.

what to knock off the bottom of those lists and how to say no to those things that don't deserve a spot on your list or your calendar at all. Saying no to good things leaves room for saying yes to *great* things (and having time to do them well).

One of my favorite ways to start shaving things off my list is to do a brain dump of everything floating around in my head that I believe I can or should do (more on lists in the next chapter). Then I identify roughly a third of the things on the list that are lowest priority. Those are usually the things that have been in my brain to do for a while and keep getting carried over without getting done from list to list. Then for each of those bottom-third items I ask myself:

What is the worst thing that would happen if I never do this?

Is there any other way for this to get done without my doing it?

Is there any way for me to half-do this and move on from it?

These questions can get you thinking about how to delegate, how to streamline what you're working on, and how to cut corners where possible. For example, after my family and I moved into our new house, my home office was pretty empty and I thought pleasing decor might be a good idea. I thought it might provide a nicer backdrop for when I worked by videoconference. So, *Decorate office* kept coming up every single time I made a list. But it kept not being a priority, because I had a lot of other things going on (remember three kids under four and a move?). So I asked myself:

What would be the worst thing that happened if I never did this? Probably nothing. I'd have a plain little room that hardly anyone ever entered but me and I wouldn't have the most interesting video call backdrop.

Is there any other way for it to get done? That got me thinking that maybe I could hire a decorator to do it. I started looking into options to delegate the task of decorating the office at a reasonable price.

Or could I *half* do it and move on? It hadn't gotten done because I was trying to make the room perfectly themed and decorated when just throwing some bookshelves and framed prints together might work just fine. Perfection can be the enemy of progress. Would anyone know the difference? I could set a timer and use just one hour to order decor, then two hours on the weekend to build and hang that decor. I could delegate part of the job (assembling the bookshelves and hanging framed prints) to someone else who would be glad to help—like my dad, who happens to be both handy and retired with extra time. Maybe I could get a satisfactory amount done in a little bit of time. And that would be good enough and much better than no decoration at all.

All of these options are ways of clearing items off my own list of priorities, but still closing the loop and completing the task. Even deciding *not* to decorate at all is an option. It means I've made a decision and can stop letting it linger in my brain and clutter my lists. (For reference, I went with the "half-do it and move on" method and my office looks great now—thanks to my dad's help!)

HOW MUCH IS MY TIME WORTH?

One of my former managers at Google, Anas Osman, VP, Strategy and Operations at Google Cloud, taught me a great deal about the value of time. He had a crystal-clear image of how much his time was worth. When I noticed he was always cutting it close for flights, he said, "If you're not missing five percent of your flights, you're spending too much of your life in an airport!" He was traveling round-trip about thirty weeks a year, so by getting to the airport "right on time" and not a minute sooner for those flights, he was saving himself about sixty hours of time. Missing around three flights a year (5 percent of thirty round-trip flights) was certainly less of an inconvenience than sixty hours sitting in an airport! Not everyone would agree with his approach to air travel, but the deeper sentiment—being picky about how you spend your time—is an important insight.

Perhaps the best piece of advice he gave me is that you should always have in mind a dollar amount of how much your time is worth. Most people assume that means how much money per hour they make at work. But that's not all he meant. It's more about how much you would pay for an hour of your time to *not* do something you *don't enjoy doing.* If you could get home to your family an hour earlier, how much would you pay to change that flight? How much would you pay for new furniture to arrive preassembled? If painting a room really would take you a full day, how much would you be willing to pay for someone else to paint for you? (Now, if you enjoy painting, that's a different story and affects the value. So it has to be something you don't particularly want to do!)

Let's go back to the example of my home office. Let's suppose that it would take me five hours to shop and install home office items. Based on this estimate, I should know what it would be worth to me to hire a full-service decorator—if I know the average value of my time per hour to do something I don't really want to do. The number can change based on your current priorities at work or home, your financial situation, or the flexibility of your schedule, but it's a number you should be able to name without too much thought.

One of my friends was hand-washing her baby bottles and small pieces at the end of every day and I asked her why she didn't just put them in the dishwasher. She said because she wouldn't have the bottles ready in time to make them the night before for the next day, and she didn't have enough bottles to do both. So (because I'm *that* annoying productivity friend) I asked her how long it took to hand-wash and dry the bottles and all their pieces every night. She estimated about fifteen to twenty minutes. I started doing the math in my head and realized that she was spending over 120 hours (or fifteen work days!) a year washing bottles!

All to save about $50 or the average cost of a new set of eight baby bottles. In this situation it would be helpful for her to know how much her time was worth an hour, multiplied by 120 hours, and to compare that to the cost of buying new bottles. Unless she values her time at less than $0.41/ hour, or enjoys washing bottles, she's probably better off buying a new set for the year she'd be using them.

Arguments could be made for finding joy in washing the bottles, multitasking by listening to a podcast or other activity while doing the hand-washing, or for not wanting an extra set of bottles with limited cabinet storage space. But for the sake of this example, it's certainly worth considering the value of her time for an activity she performs daily.

It's important to think of your time as the *most* valuable resource. And when a task comes up that you aren't sure is worth the value of your time, here are a few questions to ask yourself that help clarify whether it's worth it:

QUESTION	ACTION
Do I like doing this task?	If so, I can be a little looser on the value of my time.
Will it take too much effort to delegate it?	If it'll take me three hours to find, talk to, walk through, and teach someone else how to do something that would take me two hours to do myself, it's not worth it to delegate.
Is there something I'd *much* rather be doing instead?	If so, pay or delegate this activity to someone else.
Is my time much more valuable elsewhere?	If you are paid hourly and could be making more money spending your time doing that job and paying someone to do the task at hand, do that instead.

Do I feel like I "should" do it?	Even though you could pay or delegate someone to do this for you, completing this task brings you a sense of pride and ownership, so you can continue to do it.
Can someone else do it **much** better?	Even if you have the time to do the task, it might still be worthwhile to delegate or pay others so the result is what you want.
If someone asked me to do this tomorrow, how much would I pay out of my own pocket to do *nothing* instead during that time?	Decide how much it's worth to you to *not* do the activity and use that amount to help decide if you should delegate and how much you'd pay.

WHAT ARE YOU SAYING NO TO?

Saying **yes** to something is always
saying **no** to something else.

Many people feel stressed about saying no and feel the need to say yes because of social pressure, or the fear of disappointing others. In these cases, it's important to remember that time is a finite resource. Take the lens that every time you say yes, you're also saying no to something else (even if it's not outright). If your mother asks you to come to dinner every Friday, you may agree because you feel uncomfortable saying no. By saying yes to weekly dinner at your mom's, you're preemptively saying no to other invitations that may not have even be extended yet (this is why I try to do an annual *No-Plans November*: making no plans until the morning of for the whole month to see how my life changes when I do only what

I'm in the mood to do *that day*). By saying yes to a weekly meeting, you're saying no to work that would have been done during that slot each week (which might be okay, but you want to consciously recognize what you're giving up every week going forward!).

Yes to a new committee is *no* to time on other projects. *Yes* to a mentoring opportunity is *no* to extra time with others on your team. *Yes* to an after-work commitment is *no* to dinner with your family. In the case of dinner, you're not explicitly saying no (your children likely didn't *ask* you to come to dinner), but you're now saying no to them, because you've chosen to do something else. You've said no indirectly (which is fine if it's the right trade-off!). But every *yes* is a *no* to something else, whether that's a direct *no* or an indirect *no*. By staying aware of what that "something else" might be, you can consciously make choices about the balance of your time.

SHAVING DOWN CURRENT RESPONSIBILITIES: LAUNCH AND ITERATE

When I started coaching executives at Google I made my sessions open to anyone at the director or above job levels. Requests poured in and I found I was spending a lot of my time in coaching sessions. I was helping a lot of people, but I was feeling drained. I wasn't finding a lot of time for my other two priorities: scalable learning at Google and consulting on Google Workspace product features. I wasn't opening many new loops. I made the tough decision to limit my coaching to VPs only, which significantly reduced my number of sessions (and made some people unhappy).

I did have the actual time for these director sessions to land on my calendar, but I wasn't doing a great job with preparation and follow-up for each session. I wasn't coming up with new ideas to share or resources to help support my sessions. I was exhausted. By limiting my coaching to a smaller number of executives, I actually gave myself more breathing room to come up with an excellent, scalable group training for directors.

I was able to provide better information and share it with all of them. Furthermore, my VP sessions were more focused and impactful. This is a great example of needing more downtime, not more appointments on my calendar, to be a better worker. By doing less, I was *accomplishing* more.

When dropping a current project or commitment, it can help to think of it as temporary. Try saying *no* to something *temporarily* in order to see if it's the right decision for rebalancing your energy and schedule. Use the "launch and iterate" model:

For one month, I will try doing VP sessions only, see how I feel, and then check back in and go from there.

For one week, I will see what it's like to leave work right at 5:00 p.m., and then see how stressed I'm feeling about my work later that night after I've peeled myself away.

For one quarter, I'm going to make my team meeting every other week instead of weekly and see what that does to our decision-making speed and connection.

The purpose of this approach is to launch a potential solution for a trial period, get feedback on its effectiveness, and then iterate accordingly. Each effort gives you new data to refine the approach.

You can't always radically change your commitments (for example, it's not ideal to quit a board you joined for a two-year term after one year), but you can flag those things so that next time your seat goes up, you have the foresight to relieve yourself of that priority as you continue to balance your schedule and time.

Sometimes people tell me, *Well, I have eight hours of meetings a day and every one of them is important!* But there is always a way to start looking at your priorities as things that are really good versus things that are great. Imagine your manager just told you that you're taking on a really great project that will use approximately 25 percent of your time. Ask yourself, what *good* and still important things are you doing now that you would drop to make room for that *great* thing? Whatever comes to mind is usually the "low-hanging fruit" that you can possibly move or consolidate in your schedule.

If you're feeling like everything falls under "important" and you're not sure how to shave down your workload or schedule, it can also be helpful to get your manager or team lead involved. If you are in five project groups and you feel like you should drop two, confer with your manager about which ones are most important. You may find out that your manager doesn't care about the one committee you think matters most and you'll feel empowered to know that they may be supportive, and even encouraging, of dropping something to make room for your best work on other things.

FIVE WAYS TO SAY NO TO INCOMING REQUESTS

It's more difficult to drop current responsibilities (more about that in Chapter 6) than to say no to new requests, but declining new requests still takes a strategy. For many of us, including me, saying no does not come naturally. I had to learn—over time and with a lot of trial and error—the best way to do this. I wanted to find the balance between protecting my time and maintaining the respect and relationships I had with others. By saying no to too much, or in the wrong way, you can certainly affect social capital. It's a careful balance. These are the five tactics that work best for me and *exactly* how they look in practice:

1. **Ask more questions.** Get more details, find out what else would be helpful to know before making a decision on this. Ask all possible questions.
   - **Understand the time commitment.** *"Hi! Thanks for asking me to join this new project. Can you give more information on approximately how much time commitment this would be a week?"*
   - **See if it aligns with your top three priorities.** *"Thanks for the opportunity to join this new cross-team initiative you're working on!*

Can you share what a successful completion of this project would look like and what goals you're trying to achieve?"

- **Understand expectations and how others prioritize this assignment.** *"Thanks for the invitation to speak to your group! Can you let me know how many people would be invited, what their general roles are, and where/how you plan to promote this talk beforehand to increase attendance? Do you have examples of previous talks or events you've organized in the past and their attendance rates?"*

2. **Say you'll think about it or don't respond right away.** This is one of my all-time favorites and can be paired with option 1 to ask more questions. Sometimes I fall into the video game trap—a hyper-in-the-moment response mode where I feel I must respond instantly and definitively to every email, question, or request that comes my way. My initial reaction is to either eagerly accept or preemptively decline. Both can be detrimental. It never fails that twenty-four hours later I have a gut feeling of what I should have said or done—and many times it's the opposite. One of my favorite things to do is to read something that comes into my inbox or listen to a proposal from someone and then let it go without immediately deciding what I am going to do with it.

   - **Buy yourself time.** *"It was great to hear about the new tool you're working on and where you'd like my help. I'm going to think about it and get back to you with the level of commitment I can provide, if any."*
   - **Share your thought process.** *"Hi! Just reviewing some of my speaking requests and after thinking about it, unfortunately, I don't think I'll have time for this, given some of my current priorities. Best of luck with the event!"*

I've learned to implement this strategy with my kids. Previously, when my daughter asked me "Can I do glitter?" my knee-jerk reaction was always no, because . . . glitter. Then on a slow, rainy Sunday, when I did have time to help her and clean up, I thought, why didn't I just say yes and let her do it? Conversely, I would say "sure" to Play-Doh too fast without thinking, only to realize that we're actually leaving the house in five minutes and it's way too much work to get it all out and clean it all up. So even with my own kids I've learned to say, "Let me think about it and let you know in a minute." By that time I have moved past my gut reaction and rationally thought through my decision.

3. **Imagine the two scenarios: Yes and No.** This one can be extremely helpful for a long-term project or commitment request. I close my eyes and imagine how things would play out if I said yes, and if I said no. For example, let's say someone has asked me to travel to be part of an executive summit as a speaker. I imagine myself the day before, getting ready for the flight. What am I thinking? *I wish I hadn't signed up for this. I always have so many other things going on the last week of the quarter!* Or I imagine seeing a picture or snippet of the speaker list from the summit after saying no. Am I thinking, *I should have been on that list, I regret turning that down?* Perhaps I imagine myself on the flight on the way home. Am I thinking, *Wow that was such a good use of my time! I made so many great connections?* Sometimes just putting yourself in the shoes of that Future You on both sides of the situation can help you get a feel for which one seems more realistic, therefore helping you decide how to respond.

4. **No, but . . .** This is one of my favorite ways to say no to a request. It's a good way of saying no but not flat-out refusing something. For instance, if you think that something is worth your time to email about, but not to have a meeting about, you don't have to say no altogether to a meeting request. You can shift to another option that works better for you.

- **Preempt with email.** *"Hey! Do you mind sending over your questions first via email then we can decide if we need a meeting to discuss?"*
- **Preempt with virtual comments.** *"Hey! Do you mind starting with some of these comments in our file and we can meet if we can't resolve there?"*
- **Divert/delegate to someone else.** *"I wish I could speak at your team event but unfortunately don't have the bandwidth right now! However I have some self-led training modules on my site, or feel free to reach out to person X, who also does these trainings!"*

This way of saying no makes the person feel supported and respected, but still protects your time and priorities. You may even go the extra mile and set a reminder for yourself to check back in with them on how the event went.

5. **No, because . . .** The simplest way (and the most difficult for many of us) is to straight-up say no and explain why. Giving the additional context about what you're doing with your time and priorities helps the requestor feel like you're letting them in and not pushing them away. This could look like:
   - **No time.** *"Thanks for sharing this new initiative with me! Looks like a great opportunity. I wish I could but unfortunately I'm blocking my calendar for a few things that will likely come up this quarter. Look forward to seeing the final product!"*
   - **Your participation would be superfluous.** *"Hi! I won't be attending this meeting because I see that Amy from my team has more context on this and she's already confirmed as an attendee!"*
   - **Other priorities.** *"Hi! I won't be attending this conference because I'm using this week to work on a few heads-down items with deadlines at the end of the month but I wish you the best of luck with the content!"*

MAKE IT AN EASY YES

Once you've mastered the power of no, you can also use similar strategies in reverse. If you're trying to get someone to buy into your project or to join you, you can use these tactics *in reverse*. When I'm trying to get someone to say yes to a collaborative project or support, I think about why I say no to things and why I say yes to things. This can look like:

- **Explain how the ask aligns with their priorities:** *"Hi! I read through your public priorities for the quarter [at Google these are called OKRs—Objectives and Key Results] and found one that aligns perfectly with something I'm working on as well. I'd love to work together to achieve one of your goals for the quarter in alignment with a project I've started."*
- **Give as much detail/flexibility as possible up front.** *"Hi! I'd love for you to speak to my team. Here are more details that might help make your decision":*
  - *Date* (give multiple options if possible)
  - *Time* (give multiple options if possible)
  - *Number of people*
  - *Structure of the talk* (Q&A, presentation, give multiple options so they can pick one that sounds most appealing)
  - *Why we're asking you specifically*
  - *What success would look like for this event*

Whether you're saying no yourself or trying to get someone to say yes to you, these real-life tactics can be beneficial in getting exactly what you want out of your time or others' time.

In time and with practice, these techniques for saying no and (more importantly) protecting your time will become second nature. You'll know which tasks deserve your full attention and energy, which ones you can delegate, and which you can let go of altogether. You'll be able to avoid the guilt that can come with turning things down and the regret that often sets in when you realize you've said yes (and sometimes even no) too quickly. Learning to say *no* clears your desk and your calendar for organizing the things you say *yes* to. And setting boundaries and working norms from the start will make it less likely that you'll have to say no at all! (More on this in Chapter 12.)

PRODUCTIVITY PRACTICES

- Pick something that's sitting in your inbox or weighing on you that you'd like to say no to.
- Decide which of the "five ways to say no" is most suitable for solving the problem.
- Draft the perfect response that will help you remain respected by the requestor and keep your precious time and priorities intact.

Chapter

3

THE LIST FUNNEL

Now that you've set your priorities and protected time in your schedule by saying no, you need a way to keep track of those high-impact tasks *and* to decide exactly when to complete them on your calendar. In come lists. List-making represents the *Consolidate* part of the *5 C's of Productivity*. You're taking all the loops you have and grouping them together so you have access to them in the right place at the right time to close them.

Making lists is always associated with high levels of productivity. A renowned study by Gail Matthews at the Dominican University of California showed that writing down goals increased the likelihood of achieving them by 42 percent. While lists can be extremely helpful, they can also be tricky. How can *learn piano someday* and *finish presentation that's due by 5:00 p.m.* both show up on a list of to-do's? Although they're both things you want to do, they have completely different time frames and effort levels. One is a big-picture vision and one is something that needs to happen now—so how do they coexist?

Lists are not a one-time thing—they're a living, breathing system that makes it easier for your brain to manage tasks and ensures that you execute them. They're the backbone of productivity. Lists can help manage your life if used the right way. They can keep you honest about what you need to do and when you need to do it. They give you a level of trust with yourself that nothing is "slipping through the cracks." They free up your brain for other things. A little bit of planning can make a huge difference in how much you're getting done in the long run. In *Eat That Frog! 21 Ways to Stop Procrastinating and Get More Done in Less Time*, Brian Tracy says that spending ten to twelve minutes planning your day "will save you up to two hours (100 to 120 minutes) in wasted time and diffuse effort throughout the day." Just think of making a grocery list. If I spend five minutes making a list of what I need and writing it out organized by aisle, then twenty minutes shopping, that is more efficient than the forty minutes or so it would take me wandering around the store trying to remember the items I need and where they are. The five minutes of sitting down to plan upfront actually saved me fifteen overall minutes in the long run.

You can think of to-do lists like a funnel: start with the highest level of everything you could possibly do, or want to do, and narrow it down into what you actually will do hour by hour, based on time, energy, and priorities. The following List Funnel is something I've taught successfully at Google for years. If you find yourself keeping track of things in your head, managing the mental load of personal and work to-do's, coming out of meetings with follow-ups, constantly trying to remember things that need to get done, and juggling action items from multiple places, the

LIST FUNNEL

MAIN LIST

WEEKLY LIST

DAILY LIST

HOUR-BY-HOUR
PLAN

List Funnel is for you. You can use just pieces of the List Funnel or the whole thing. Move as far down the List Funnel as you feel you need to, based on your role, level, or responsibilities, but it is an end-to-end system for keeping track of all your to-do's. People have used this system to create their own notebooks, whiteboards, and reusable templates. Every one of them follows up to let me know how this method has saved them time and made them more productive.

MOVING DOWN THE LIST FUNNEL

The List Funnel demonstrates how effective list-making goes from macro to micro. It begins with the Main List, which you might think of as a view from thirty thousand feet of everything you have going on—a scan of every loop in your brain that hasn't been closed—without time specifications or schedules. Remember, there is no "work you" and "personal you." That's why the Main List encompasses both types of to-do's. One brain, one list. Once you've created your Main List, it feeds action items into your Weekly List. The Weekly List itemizes the specific things you are going to do off the Main List that week, assigning specific days to do them. The Daily List is an outline of your day, including the most important priorities, when you'll accomplish them, and tracking of habits you'd like to include daily. A piece of the Daily List is the Hour-by-Hour Plan, a run-through of exactly how your day will go and when every task or action will be performed that day. If you accomplish each Hour-by-Hour as planned, you accomplish all of your larger to-do's one piece, one hour at a time. These lists can all be pen-to-paper (my preference) or virtual. Both physical and digital resources for these lists can be found on my website. The most important thing is that they all exist and interact.

The Main List

At all times you should have what I call the Main List. Mine is a physical list on a notepad, but you could also keep a digital list. (Tip: Anytime you do make a physical list, make it a habit to immediately take a picture of it so if you lose the piece of paper, not all is lost!)

What you'll notice about the Main List is that it's divided into specific types of energy/action, based on all the things you need to do, almost like a dashboard. My example here separates work tasks from personal ones, and then organizes them by the *type* of action necessary to accomplish them. By breaking it up this way, it helps you have an easy place to go when, for instance, you have a long flight during which you can use

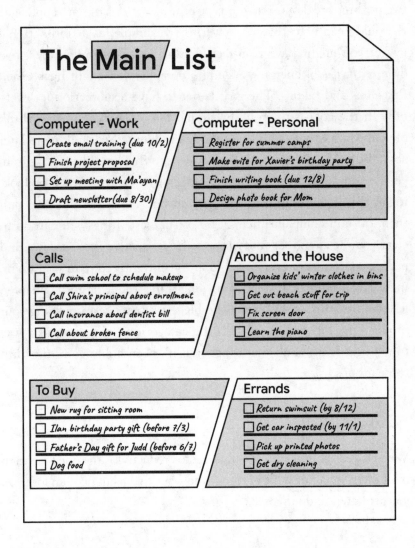

The Main / List

Computer - Work
- [ ] Create email training (due 10/2)
- [ ] Finish project proposal
- [ ] Set up meeting with Ma'ayan
- [ ] Draft newsletter (due 8/30)

Computer - Personal
- [ ] Register for summer camps
- [ ] Make evite for Xavier's birthday party
- [ ] Finish writing book (due 12/8)
- [ ] Design photo book for Mom

Calls
- [ ] Call swim school to schedule makeup
- [ ] Call Shira's principal about enrollment
- [ ] Call insurance about dentist bill
- [ ] Call about broken fence

Around the House
- [ ] Organize kids' winter clothes in bins
- [ ] Get out beach stuff for trip
- [ ] Fix screen door
- [ ] Learn the piano

To Buy
- [ ] New rug for sitting room
- [ ] Ilan birthday party gift (before 7/3)
- [ ] Father's Day gift for Judd (before 6/7)
- [ ] Dog food

Errands
- [ ] Return swimsuit (by 8/12)
- [ ] Get car inspected (by 11/1)
- [ ] Pick up printed photos
- [ ] Get dry cleaning

your computer but can't make phone calls. Or for when you know you're doing things around the house and you won't be on your computer. Or you're already out running errands and find yourself with extra time before school pickup. It's you setting up Future You for complete success by having a place to go where similar actions are grouped.

These are the six standard categories I use but you can use your own—anything that can be grouped together for the same type of action. Most of my work is on the computer but you could certainly have two or three breakouts for your type of work actions if that's applicable (I would keep it to three or fewer). For example, as a transactional lawyer you might have *Contract Drafting* and *Negotiation Prep*, two different types of energies. As a photographer you might have *Client Responses* and *Editing*. The goal is not to have a subsection for every project; the goal is to group by similar *type* of work. For now, think of your Main List as your one-time brain dump. We'll talk more later about how new things make their way onto this list (like to-do's from emails and meeting action items) and how it evolves. You'll be looking at this list weekly and crossing items off of it each time you pull them off and complete them. One of the best things you can do to clear your head and set yourself up to be productive is to sit down and make a Main List of every open loop you currently have in your brain, including deadlines. If you do only one thing from this entire chapter, it should be this. It will make the biggest difference in pushing your productivity forward. Start with the categories listed above as a way to jog your brain of all the things that it's been holding on to within these groups.

The Weekly List

When asked about the biggest obstacle to productivity, the one I mention most often is having a list of things you want to do, but no plan for *when* you actually will do them.

One exec I met with complained of having a never-ending to-do list with items that just kept carrying over. I asked her to bring her list to our first coaching session. I also printed her calendar. We sat down and went through each item of her list and I said, *"Okay, looks like you want to get this done, when do you plan to do it?"* For almost all the items, her answer was *"Well, I'm not sure because I have meetings all day and no time here or here so . . . maybe at night?"* No one wants to do all their work at night, especially after being in meetings all day—that's what leads to burnout. We have to consider our to-do items as *part* of our weekly schedule and block time for them just as we do for meetings.

At the beginning of each week (make it a Sunday night or Monday morning tradition) you take a look at your Main List and from it make a Weekly List. It's too distracting to work from only your Main List because you're using energy points to look at things you have no intention of doing that week (more on list workflow later in the chapter).

After making your Weekly List, take a look at your schedule for the week. Now fill in the pieces of how you plan to "close" these loops. Remember, the Main List is everything you want to get done *eventually*, so if this is a busy week of travel or meetings, it's okay that some things won't come off that list and make it onto your week. I like to take the parts of my Main List and create obvious spots/themes for those every week. Friday early evening, I run errands. Wednesday night, I do personal tasks on my computer. Tuesday evening I don't touch my computer and just do physical things around my house. Sunday night I shop online for anything I need. This helps ensure that each area of my Main List gets addressed at least once a week.

One component of peak productivity is
having a good inventory of everything
you're not doing yet. That is equally as
important as everything you are doing.

You might notice when you're looking at your calendar, you're not seeing an obvious place that week where you have time to put work blocks for your to-do items. This indicates that you either need to 1) be realistic about what you can accomplish, given your travel/meeting schedule, or 2) start making room on your calendar for these items. Careful attention to your Weekly List will keep you from being surprised at the end of the workweek when you haven't completed intended tasks and then end up working all weekend or find yourself behind the next week. We'll talk more in the next chapter about tracking the ebb and flow of your productive energy, which can help you figure out where different types of work belong in your schedule.

You also see a section in your Weekly List to list some of those daily themes. As mentioned, this can help you manage your energy and workload in the long run, and on a week-by-week short-term basis. Let's say you're cooking dinner every single night. How daunting is it to start that process each day with *What should I cook for dinner?* Imagine you had themes instead, like meatless Monday, Italian food Tuesday, new recipe Wednesday, soup night Thursday, etc. Themes make planning and executing dinner much easier, ensure you're trying out new recipes frequently, and prevent you from eating Italian food three nights in a row (which *actually* might not be such a bad thing).

Similarly, theming your days at work ensures you're focusing on all of your priorities every week, and not forgetting to check in on any one thing for weeks at a time. You could make Thursday "Administrative tasks and expenses day" and Friday "Client follow-up." The themes should mostly stay consistent week over week when you make your Weekly List, so they become patterns. You can build your themes based on things already going on that day—if you hold the staff meeting for your team on Mondays, maybe that day's theme is "People Management" and you also schedule your individual meetings with reports later that day. You could also build your themes based on the blocks of your Main List. Themes can occasionally change based on travel and other commitments. This consistency helps when you have unexpected free time

The Weekly List

Top 3 priorities this week — When I plan to do this

☐ Finish project proposal ~2 hrs	Day Tuesday morning
☐ Register kids for summer camps - 1hr	Day Wednesday evening
☐ Draft newsletter for manager - 30mins	Day Thursday morning

Other things I can get to this week — When I plan to do this

☐ Return bathing suits at mall	Day Friday afternoon
☐ Go through kids' winter clothes	Day Tuesday evening
☐ Call Marie's principal about enrollment	Day Thursday at lunch break
☐ Make evite for Xavier's birthday	Day Wednesday evening
☐ Order party favors for school party	Day Sunday evening
☐ Organize bathroom cabinet	Day Sunday evening
☐ Video chat with Mom	Day Friday morning
☐ Sign up for family camping trip	Day Wednesday evening

Themes for each day
S Grocery & Food Prep
M Work Plan & Prep/Laundry
T Coaching Sessions/House Projects
W Project/Personal Computer Work
T Admin Tasks/Yard Work
F Emails & Follow Up/Errands
S Rest & Fun

Habit tracker
Meditate ○○○○○
Workout ○○○○○
Nature Walk ○○○○○

Looking ahead
Anything next week I need to be thinking about

Board meeting for 501c3 is next week

on a certain day because you can instantly refer to your theme and know what to work on.

The Weekly List is where you specify the things you can do this week from your Main List, and when you will do them. If you're in a meeting and you get an action item that has to be finished this week, and know you won't get to it today, it should be added to the Weekly List. The

Weekly List also has a spot to track habits you're trying to build, like meditation or exercise. The Weekly List helps drive the creation of your Daily List for each day.

The Daily List

The Daily List brings it all together. It's the WHEN. It's the go-to place for you to check every day. Some people I've worked with at Google make laminated Daily List sheets, which they fill out every night with dry-erase markers. Others have turned their whiteboard into a large Daily List template. Many like to make it a digital file that they update daily. Whatever your preference, the Daily List captures the nitty-gritty and shows individual tasks and meetings that will come together for you to get more done.

The first section is focused on your absolute top priority: What task do you *have* to get done each day? Until that item is finished, everything else is a distraction. Our natural tendency is to pick the "easier" small things to do first because it takes less of our energy to start those. But also in *Eat That Frog!*, Brian Tracy talks about the benefit of doing your most difficult/important task first if possible. This way, you ride the accomplishment of that for the rest of the day rather than operating under the weight of that unmet responsibility. When I go on a walk in my neighborhood it's a pleasant route, with one hill. When I go left, the hill is at the beginning of the route; when I go right, it comes toward the end. Anytime I go right I'm thinking the whole time that I still have this huge hill I have to get over! When I go left and get it over with right away, I feel accomplished already and enjoy the rest of the walk.

The list of *Other priorities* comes directly from your Weekly List. What did you commit to doing for that day? What falls into each day's theme that you can fit in? If you're finding it overwhelming to make this list, imagine that someone came to you and told you that you have to leave for a month-long vacation tomorrow or else you lose your vacation time. What would you make *sure* you got done before you left? Make that your starting point.

If you had a meeting in the morning and an action was assigned to

The Daily List

Top priority today

Finish project proposal!

Today I'm grateful for:

Sister coming over for dinner!

Other priorities:

- ☐ Respond to Bhavna about 2025 budget
- ☐ Kids' winter clothes
- ☐ Set up coaching sessions for next week
- ☐
- ☐
- ☐
- ☐

Hour by hour 🕐

7am	Laura 30 & make breakfast
8am	School drop off/commute/sort email
9am	Finish project proposal
10am	Finish project proposal
11am	Respond emails and review coaching session request form
12pm	Lunch & walk
1pm	Meeting
2pm	Meeting
3pm	Send Bhavna 2025 budget/Read email folder
4pm	Meeting/Revisit email folder
5pm	Commute home/start dinner
6pm	Dinner & play time w/ kids
7pm	Go through kids' winter clothes

Snack-size to-do's

Order more dog food

Call contractor about paint color

Mindful Moments

- Closed email once to work ●
- Spent 30min in silence ○
- Nature walk ○
- ○

Tomorrow's priorities

you that needs to be completed by end of day, add it immediately to your *Other priorities* on your Daily List. Most importantly, every item on this *Other priorities* list should have a place on your Hour-by-Hour Plan. *If it's on your list, it's on your calendar.* The Hour-by-Hour Plan should also include anything like a commute, a workout, meetings, time to check and process email (more on email in Chapter 16), and any other commitments. Imagine it as a dress rehearsal of how your day will go. It can be a physical list (I prefer this, something about writing it down really makes it stick) or blocks on your virtual calendar. Your day might not always go exactly as planned, but it will *definitely* never go as planned if there is no plan.

You'll also notice a spot for a few snack-size to-do's. These are small individual to-do's or pieces of your larger action items that take five minutes or less and can be done during those unscheduled breaks that come up during your day. They can also be things that come up throughout the day that need to be done by end of day. If you realize in the morning that you need to make a quick call to your landlord before the day is out—add it directly to your snack-size to-do's. Then, if a meeting ends early, go straight to this list and make that one quick phone call. Did one of your other tasks take less time than you expected? Place that quick online order for that one thing you needed. Having snack-size to-do's readily available ensures that every minute of your day is used well and keeps you from using any in-between time just trying to figure out "what to do next."

At the end of the Daily List is a chance for you to catch items that weren't completed that need to carry over to the next day and to cross anything that did get completed off your Weekly List. This step is so important to make sure that you didn't commit to do something one day, not get to it, only to lose it out of your system. Things don't get crossed off the higher list on the List Funnel until they're completely done, making sure you're reminded of them in list review if they still need to be completed. I fill out the Daily List for the following day the night before (more in Chapter 12 on why this is important). You'll also see a section to write something you're grateful for. I find that this adds perspective. As I'm moving through my day and through my to-do's, I love looking up to the top of my list and remembering something that makes me happy that day.

Other Lists

There are other uses for lists that aren't referenced here. These are ancillary and should exist outside of your regular List Funnel because they have a different workflow.

Capture List

We rarely think of our best ideas when we're sitting in front of our lists or in front of our computers. We think of them in the shower, on our commute, or while walking the dog. You'll recognize *Capture* as one of the 5 *C's of Productivity* from the introduction. The Capture List is what helps bridge an open loop to a closed loop because it's where you write down any loop that opens in your brain. Think of it as a parking lot or holding ground to keep things that come to you until you can fully sort them onto a section of your Main List. So often we tell ourselves to "make a mental note" of something, but too many mental notes leave our brain overwhelmed and on the hook for too many things. Instead, make a real note.

The two most important aspects of the Capture List are 1) that it is easily accessible anywhere (typically on your mobile phone and on your computer) and 2) that you can add things using a voice dictation function. Your Capture List should be a hodge-podge of things you've thought of and will include all different types of actions that need to be sorted. Anything from *"Call Juliet's school about absence next week,"* to *"Email landlord re: landscaping,"* to *"Buy new lightbulb for porch light."* All of these things are random thoughts of things you need or want to do and, for now, will be noted all in the same place. One brain, one Capture List. Then, when you pull up your Main List each week, reference your Capture List to transfer these items to the correct part of your Main List (more on moving through this list workflow later in the chapter).

One of the best uses of a Capture List I've ever seen is by Lorraine Twohill, SVP of Global Marketing at Google. She uses Google Keep to capture anything that inspires her creatively. Whether it is an advertisement, a picture, a quote, or something she thought of spontaneously that she'd like to do, she never lets an idea or creative thought get away from her. As soon as it enters her mind, she gives it a home on her Capture List. This becomes her reference point for future visions and executions and serves as the place to collect and digest anything that has inspired her lately.

"Collection" Lists

This is a list of things or places that you'd like to get to someday, read someday, work on someday, or travel to someday, but won't necessarily be part of your day-to-day to-do's. For example, maybe you have a list of books you want to read, piano songs you want to learn, or recipes you want to try. We'll talk more about how to make time for routines like reading and playing piano in future chapters, but that type of list would be outside of your Main List, can be kept in addition to it, and is checked in on in a similar cadence (monthly) or when needed (when you finish a book and need a new one).

Grocery List

It would be a little cumbersome to add every single grocery item you needed to your Main List *To Buy* section. Instead, keep a separate Grocery List that lives in a place that's always accessible. Ideally this list is kept on your mobile device, synced with your computer, shared with your spouse/partner/roommate, and accessible by voice dictation (so when your hand is dirty cracking your last egg you can verbally add "eggs" to your Grocery List). Before I go to the grocery store each week I take a look at my digital Grocery List, then recopy everything I need into a list broken out by store section (*Produce, Dairy, Meat, Grain, Frozen, Aisles, Snacks, Beverages*), then take a picture! Or if I stop by the store unexpectedly, I can also pull up the Grocery List on my phone and see what my husband and I have added that I can pick up quickly. (You can also access my Grocery List template on my site.)

THE LIST FUNNEL WORKFLOW

A good list workflow is what takes productivity to the next level. It can take a little bit of time up front to make your one-time Main List, but after that, you need only a few minutes each day and week to maintain this

system. You can see how this would look every week in the image below.
For the most part, the Main List itself stays consistent as items come and
go. If you have a digital Main List, you can simply remove items as you
circle back during your weekly review and if you have a physical Main
List you can simply recopy it over once a month or so when enough items
have been crossed off that you want to start on a fresh paper. Then every
week (Sunday night or Monday morning) you make a Weekly List and a
Daily List for each day and pull items off of your Capture List. While
each of these workflows may look like they take time, they're really only
a few minutes or less. Build them into your schedule and workflow and
they'll become second nature. Lists can be standalone but it's the workflow that makes them a system. Having a standard workflow where you
trust yourself to look at your lists on a specific cadence eliminates such a
stress about "deadlines" because you're ahead of them. If I have a project

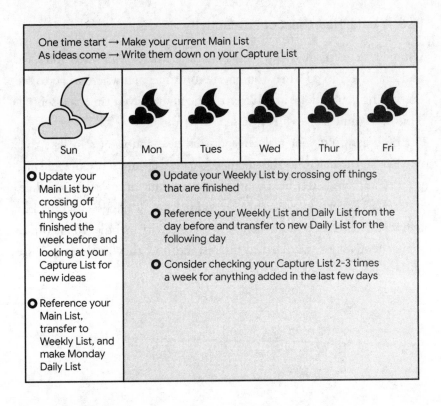

that's due in two months on my Master List, I'll presumably see that *eight* or more times when I look at the Master List once each week—the deadline won't sneak up on me and I'll make sure I have allotted time for it before "the last minute." A schedule using the List Funnel to create a seamless workflow would look something like the one on the facing page.

Depending on how much you're "on the go," you may find that you need to transfer items from your Capture List to your Main List more often, maybe two or three times a week or even every evening when you're making your Daily List for the following day. If you think of something while you're sitting right next to your Main List, there's no need for the additional step of adding to the Capture List first—just add it directly to your Main List. Or if you think of something that you have to do that day, add it to the Daily List instead (making sure you have a time slot for it!).

Lists Are the Heartbeat of Productivity

Using lists effectively is key. Understanding where to go when you have an idea, where to go when you have extra time, and where to go to see everything you've done and haven't done at any given time is essential. This List Funnel solves all of these.

By organizing your tasks, responsibilities, and to-do's in lists that move from the macro to the micro, you gain a clearer sense of scale and priority and are better able to manage your daily and weekly schedule. It becomes easier and easier, like second nature. While lists and the List Funnel are absolutely fundamental to productivity, in order to maximize their effectiveness, we need to understand how they apply to our use of time.

PRODUCTIVITY PRACTICES

- Do a brain dump and make your current Main List.
- Use the Weekly and Daily Lists to play out a week.
- Add a Capture List on your phone (using features like Apple Notes or Google Keep) to capture any ideas or open loops that come to you that aren't already on your list.
- Add a Grocery List on your phone that you can access with the voice dictation function on a smart-home device when you're in the kitchen with your hands dirty!

PART II

When to Do It

Chapter

4

KNOW YOUR FLOW

One of my coaching clients was an advertising executive based on the West Coast. He had a team based in New York and teammates in California. I asked him when his energy was highest and he replied, "The morning! I'm definitely a morning person." So I asked, "Oh great, so you do most of your heads-down strategic work in the morning?" He replied, "No, I'm in meetings with East Coasters all morning so I actually do most of my work when I'm feeling low energy in the afternoons." You can see why he might not be feeling like his most productive self. Even though he was dedicating *some* time to do focused work, he was dedicating the *wrong* time based on his energy levels.

Even more important than *what* you plan to do is *when* you plan to do it. While everyone's schedule has some blocks of time (like meetings) that are out of our control, our blocks of free time don't all have equal

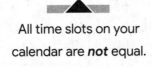

All time slots on your
calendar are *not* equal.

value. It's important to learn when is the best time for *you* to do a particular kind of task.

We all have some sense of when we're at our brightest and most energetic—when we're *in the zone*—and when we're not. When many of us began working remotely, the stripping away of commutes left room for things like midday walks and naps, or earlier or later starts, enabling us to view our personal energy flows with new clarity.

Some people are night owls and some people can function well at 5:00 a.m. It's built into our systems. Recent research, including a 2016 study conducted by the Sleep Society and published by Oxford University Press, suggests that your chronotype—your own personal circadian rhythm—is largely determined by biology. My husband and I find that we're on *exactly* opposite schedules. When I feel like I'm crashing from the day (usually around 2:00 p.m.), it's his favorite time to start a workout! I love waking up early to get ready for the day at 6:00 a.m., and he wants to talk about finances at 11:00 p.m., when I'm basically asleep. I've seen these rhythms emerging in my own children ever since they were babies. My daughter doesn't care as much about reading books at night because she's starting to get tired, but she'll happily sit and read or listen to books in the morning. Around lunchtime, she loves doing art when she's feeling her most creative. These rhythms already exist inside all of us. If we can figure out what they are, we can make the time we set aside to do things the *very best time* to do them.

CHARTING YOUR PRODUCTIVITY PATTERNS

One of the first questions I ask executives on the intake form for my coaching sessions is, *If you had an entire day tomorrow, with no meetings, no interruptions, no standing commitments, but a bunch of things to get done, how would you structure your day?* This one question can be a good starting point to figure out when your most productive times are. For some people this looks like: waking up at 9:00 a.m., slow start to the morning with emails or catching up on industry news, a walk, a late lunch, then heads-down work until 7:00 or 8:00 in the evening. Maybe starting even later with a finish around midnight. For others it might look like a 5:00 a.m. start, a midday workout, a break from 2:00 to 4:00, and some light email triage before the evening, when they are out of energy. Keep a little notepad by your desk for two weeks and any time you're feeling really productive, write down the conditions. My productivity patterns, when I feel most in the flow, seem to be:

- In the morning/early afternoon between 8:00 a.m. and 1:00 p.m.
- When no one else is in the room
- Within two hours of having coffee
- Listening to instrumental music (usually film scores)
- After I've eaten a filling meal (but not too filling)
- On a laptop, as opposed to my double screens, which offer too much opportunity to multitask

Observe when you're at your best (and worst), write it down for a few weeks, and notice patterns to gain more insight into your particular energy flow.

FINDING YOUR POWER HOURS

Once you've come up with some of your general productivity patterns, you can start mimicking your ideal conditions as often as possible. This also helps you really narrow down to find what I call your *Power Hours—the two to three hours a day that you feel your most productive*. Productive can mean different things, so for the sake of Power Hours let's talk about heads-down, focused, strategic work. This is ideally when you'd work on your individual tasks related to your top three priorities. Think of your Power Hours as the time that your energy points are best spent. It's the time that you feel most "on top of it." During these blocks of time, it would be a real waste to sit in low-energy meetings, because these hours offer your best chance at producing *your* best individual output. Mine are usually between 9:00 a.m. and 11:00 a.m.

Sometimes you find your Power Hours partially overlap with commitments you can't move during that time, such as your manager's meeting or taking your kid to school. That's okay! Try honoring these hours *to any degree*. Blocking your Power Hours for your own work, even one to three times a week, or even just one hour of your three Power Hours, will make a huge difference in how much control you feel over your work and to-do lists.

The executive I mentioned earlier started reserving two mornings a week for heads-down work only. He shifted all his East Coast meetings to the other three mornings as much as possible. He said this increased his overall weekly productivity by almost 30 percent because he knew he had these two huge blocks of time during his natural time of feeling productive. He was no longer sludging through work at his lowest-energy hours. I've been told by countless clients that *this one single shift in their schedule has made the biggest difference in their overall productivity*. Finding your Power Hours and then shifting your schedule slightly to protect them for your top three priorities can be the smallest change that makes the biggest difference. I coached one executive who was taking her lunch break every day at noon. She realized that her Power Hours were really 10:00 to 1:00 each day. She started taking a later lunch and found that the 12:00–1:00 p.m. hour was one of her most productive hours each day—and to think she used to spend it eating lunch!

WHAT TO DO IN YOUR OFF-PEAK HOURS

On the flip side of Power Hours are your one to two lowest-energy hours each day. I call these your "Off-peak Hours," not because they happen outside the business day, but because they happen outside your peak energy levels. If you're a morning person, it probably falls somewhere in the afternoon. If you're a late-afternoon person, you're probably not quite ready to power through your Daily List at 8:00 a.m. What do you do with those hours? They're an excellent place for handling other activities like catch-ups over coffee, submitting expenses, or all of those low-energy, quick-response emails.

Counterintuitive as it might seem, you're also more likely to be creative when you're lower energy. When we're less focused we are considering a larger range of ideas and connections, as our brains are a little "fuzzier." According to research by Mareike Wieth, associate professor of psychology at Albion College, we are more creative in the afternoons or other times when we are a little tired or groggy and unable to hone our focus. This is also a great time to go on a walk, which allows our mind to naturally wander even more.

It's important to remember that while our chronotype is mostly set in stone by our own biology, you want to always check in to make sure that what you're doing is working and test your assumptions about your best time to do certain tasks. While writing this book, I thought I'd write best in my Power Hours so I started by blocking those for writing every day. But as the weeks went on I found that those high-energy hours were better for outlining, reviewing edits, and making decisions about the book. Contrary to what I expected, I felt most creative and in the writing flow during my lower-energy times. I ended up adjusting my schedule and work blocks completely based on this realization.

WITH THE FLOW

Knowing your Power Hours and your Off-peak Hours each day helps you be in control. It makes the time you set aside the best time to do something. It creates better output and ensures your energy is in the right place before you attempt a task. The best way to think of this is: When am I in the mood to do this type of task? Slot it there! Hint: If you sit down at your desk to do something and you're thinking, "ugggghhhhhh," it's probably not the best time to do it. Give yourself permission to not do something you're not in the mood to do (with a good List Funnel you should be ahead of your deadlines anyway!). Ask yourself, does doing this task at this time feel like paddling against the current or floating downstream with the current? You want to feel like you're floating downstream and easily doing something when you set out to do it. That's how you know it's the best time to get it done. This knowledge gives you the permission to have low-energy times of the day and lets you use them for things that are compatible with this kind of energy, while you're maximizing your time during your most effective times of the day.

Similarly, you should feel empowered to capitalize on times when you're "in the mood" to do something. If you had blocked two hours to work on something and added a break after because you assumed you'd be drained, but you actually still feel energized and motivated to work on it, keep going! Thursday is typically my rest day during the week from working out because I'm usually tired. But occasionally I'll wake up Thursday mornings with the energy to work out and so I will, even though I didn't originally plan to! Planning for your typical productivity and energy flow makes a huge difference, but there's no time like the present to re-ask yourself what it is you *feel* like doing or not doing.

By now you've learned how to recognize and set your priorities and to identify the tasks necessary for achieving them. You've learned how to say no to things, and be friendly, but protect precious time. You've understood the absolute importance of making lists to keep track of your workflow. You've learned how to determine what hours of the day are best—for *you*—to schedule various types of work. But how on earth do you synthesize all this valuable knowledge into a calendar that works? It's easier than you might think.

PRODUCTIVITY PRACTICES

- Keep a notepad at your desk for two weeks. Anytime you're feeling in the zone—exceptionally productive—write down some of the conditions. Notice patterns.
- From there, figure out what are the two to three hours a day that you feel the most focused. Reserve those as often as possible in your schedule for tasks related to your top priorities.
- Use your Off-peak Hours for meetings, brainstorms, catch-ups, reading industry articles, or routine administrative tasks.

Chapter

5

ZERO-BASED CALENDARING

When accountants create a budget for the following year, they'll sometimes use what is called zero-based budgeting. It loosely means that we don't look at the budget or expenses from last year to estimate what we need this year. We start completely from scratch and ask ourselves, *What do we really need based on what we know today?* This mindset can be used to balance out what is called the *endowment effect*, a psychological finding that people are more likely to place value on an object they already own (or a meeting they already have on the calendar) than the same object that they do not own (if they had to accept the same meeting invite starting today). I like to apply this same principle to clearing out my clothes in what I call zero-based closeting: If my closet was a store, and I walked into it *today* to go shopping, which of these clothes would I actually buy?

This mode of thinking helps us shed the idea of keeping something because it's always been there, and instead focus on the current reality of what we truly need, *right now.* This is also the basis of what I call *Zero-based Calendaring.* It's the practice of thinking through what your ideal calendar would be if you could think through your commitments, meetings, and priorities with a fresh view. One of my favorite things in the world is the reaction when I bring someone a *completely blank calendar* and a marker. It feels like such a fresh start—a new beginning. Suddenly, it's as if they are the designer of their own life. (Spoiler alert: they are!) When I'm working with my clients, we sit down together to draft a fresh ideal template of their week if it looked exactly the way they wanted. Obviously there are things we can't move and commitments we have to keep, but we use this as a template and starting point to brainstorm your *ideal* schedule. Think of it as identifying the "building blocks" of your schedule and then you add things on top of them. Anyone can do this for themselves in a few easy steps.

With a completely blank calendar, add in this order:

1. **Things that *cannot* move.** (In a budget, you could think of this as taxes that have to be paid, the nonnegotiable.) This could be your manager's staff meeting, dropping your child off at school, or any other commitment that has *no* chance of shifting.

2. **Your Power Hours and urgent blocks.** Block when you'd like time for your own heads-down work, even if it's only one hour of your three-hour block or only one to two days a week. Any time that you can block on a weekly basis during your Power Hours is golden. You may also notice that some days' Power Hours are better than others. I know that 9:00 a.m. to 11:00 a.m. on Friday is the most powerful of all my Power Hours, because I'm motivated to crank work out before the weekend. I make *sure* to block those hours every week. This is when I slot my biggest projects and most strategic tasks. You can also use the advice from Chapter 2 and block some time every day to handle urgent matters.

3. **Your Off-peak Hours.** This can be on a recurring daily basis (times after lunch for a walk, or for emails, or to decompress; a thirty-minute morning block to read industry news—whatever you identified in

charting your productivity patterns). They can also be on a one-off or weekly basis. For example, you know that you're always needing a break after your two-hour staff meeting on Mondays, so you go ahead and block that time. Down swings can *also* be on a weekly basis. I know that on Thursday mornings I tend to feel a little overwhelmed and tired. I know I'm not alone—during the ten years I taught barre workout classes, the studio had the lowest number of class attendees on Thursdays. People had worked hard Monday through Wednesday, they weren't bearing down for the weekend yet, and they were just not into working out that day. It was a universal rest day for many. I feel the same way at work. I try to avoid having important conversations, attending decision-making meetings, starting new projects, or participating in strategic discussions on Thursdays if possible. Maybe you cook dinner for your family all week and by Thursday you're kind of over cooking and, as a result, dread that night. Make that your one night for leftovers or takeout. My daughter was taking gymnastics after school on Thursdays and I felt like she had low energy and therefore didn't love it. I switched her to a Monday afternoon class and it was an entirely different experience. Just knowing these patterns about your energy levels makes a huge difference. Planning ahead of them makes an even bigger difference.

4. **Your points of control.** These are small times throughout the week where you are planning for the rest of your time. This could look like a short Monday morning or Sunday evening block to create your Weekly List, or a ten- to fifteen-minute chunk at the end of your day to make your Daily List for the following day. Let's say your manager has a two-hour staff meeting and you know that anytime you have a meeting immediately after, you feel overwhelmed. It could be because that's a long block of time and you need a break or it could be because you always have action items that you need to process after the meeting. Either way, that thirty minutes is a point of

control—go ahead and block it! Having that thirty minutes blocked for yourself each week is going to have exponential benefits, more than having another thirty-minute spot blocked somewhere else in your week. After coaching with one executive we found that if he did not have an hour or so on Monday mornings to sort his email, make his Weekly List, and meet with his assistant, he estimated his week was at least 20 percent less effective. As I mentioned, when I was in sales, I tried to keep Monday morning for pitch/call prep, Tuesday–Thursday for weekly and one-off sales calls, and Friday for wrap-up and follow-up from pitches. Keeping this structure made sure I never showed up for a call unprepared and never dropped the ball on follow-up items.

5. **Daily themes.** As we mentioned in the Weekly List, it's helpful to have a general idea of your daily themes throughout the week. Business leaders, including Treehouse founder Ryan Carson, Thrive Global CEO and Huffington Post founder Arianna Huffington, Spotify CEO Daniel Ek, and X (Formerly Twitter) cofounder Jack Dorsey, have all used this method. Daily themes help you go deep into one topic and avoid task/content switching, or what I like to call puzzle scheduling, which is slotting in a ton of different topics and different types of meetings and switching context many times on the same day. Doctors often theme their days by having consultations Monday, surgeries Tuesday, and follow-ups Friday. A study in the *Journal of Experimental Psychology: Human Perception and Performance* indicates that switching mental gears causes time and energy to be lost and decreases effectiveness, which we can all feel after a particularly "all over the place" day.

By having declared themes (even half day themes), you are able to 1) get deeper on a topic because you've been thinking about it for longer (imagine the benefits of a project meeting, then a one-on-one with someone, then some individual work time, all on the same topic, all within the same day) and 2) ensure that you're checking in on something you care about, comprehensively, at least once a week. If I make Thursday my *Administrative task and email catch-up* day or my *Big-picture project/visioning day*, I'm sure that I won't go more than a week without touching base with those things, and Monday through Wednesday I don't stress about my administrative tasks because I know that day is coming! You can also have themes for personal tasks like Sunday: *Grocery & meal prep*; Monday: *Laundry*; Tuesday: *Around the house projects*. I have both a work theme and personal theme for each day. Another benefit of having personal themes is that you don't need to add ongoing tasks like *Laundry* to your List Funnel. You know that it's something you consistently will have to do, but you also consistently have a spot to do it (Mondays!). More to come in Chapter 17 on how to make sure you're actually doing the laundry on Monday!

What most people do (default scheduling/puzzle method)	What people should do (grouping by theme and type)
8am — Team Meeting	Morning work & Brainstorm
9am — 1:1	
10am — 1:1	
11am — dns / Leads Meeting	
12pm — Lunch	Lunch
1pm — Brainstorm	1:1 Meetings
2pm — Kick-off meeting / Call doctor	
3pm — 1:1	
4pm — Town Hall	Focus time + wrap up
5pm — Meeting	
6pm — Drive home / Dinner	
7pm — Call with APAC	

VALUE OF AN UNPLANNED DAY

While it's great to plan meetings and blocks of work time, don't underestimate the value of the occasional entirely unplanned day. If you have the ability to do a "no meeting" day on your schedule, take it! A day with no meetings or commitments at all is so different than a day with even one thirty-minute meeting at 2:00 p.m. For some reason, having even a single commitment feels more than thirty minutes' worth because your entire day still has to flow around it.

It's a good exercise to occasionally give yourself a day where you plan to work but you don't have any time commitments. It makes you feel in total control of what you need to do *and* when you want to do it, and gets you back in touch with your natural productivity patterns.

USING YOUR TEMPLATE

Now you have a template that is your starting point for your *ideal week*. You know exactly where you would slot heads-down work, you know what you want each day to roughly include, and you've made room for times when you're really focused and times when you're not. This template of building blocks becomes your starting point for each week and allows you to match your energy and focus with your tasks. So if you're looking at your Weekly List and you see that you need to really buckle down and finish something strategic, you already have some Power Hours roughly sketched out. If someone asks if you can meet in the next three weeks for a career and coffee chat, you already know your low-energy times where that would slot in nicely. If you didn't have a template, and you just told someone to *"find a free slot on my calendar!"* that coffee chat could have ended up scheduled during your Power Hours or in the thirty minutes after your staff meeting that you've already blocked for a break every week. These rough blocks of time for work and meetings are great placeholders, then more specifics come each week when you understand your workload and other things that may come up.

GRADUAL IMPLEMENTATION

> Don't think of this as blowing up the
> calendar of Current You. Think of it as
> setting up the calendar for *Future You*.

You may read this and think, *It's great to make this ideal schedule, but I can't just blow up my entire calendar and start fresh tomorrow!* Or, *I don't have this much control of my schedule; meetings just pop on my calendar or commitments come up and I have to be available!* And while it's true that there will certainly be meetings with multiple people where the only suitable block falls during one of your protected times, you want to make an informed decision about accepting that meeting—knowing exactly what you're giving up and how that will ripple-affect your schedule. By having a calendar template it can help you feel better about choosing to accept those meetings when necessary because you have other purposely blocked work time throughout the week to lean on.

You want to think of this as a rough draft of your ideal week. Your schedule will never fall 100 percent aligned to your ideal template, but it won't fall even 10 percent aligned to your ideal template if there is no template. Even one to two days of a schedule that aligns with your ideal template will feel like you're in Uptime more often.

I like to think of this as a three-months-out transition or it could be a change that coincides with another milestone like a new year or a new job. Start gradually moving meetings that you do have control over. Start slowly blocking time for low-energy work or Power Hours even if the first block is months out. Stick to those blocks and start to see how you feel when you do use high/low-energy time in the right way and go with the currents of your natural flows. Start to see how much better your work is when you're doing it at the right time, or theming your days to get the most out of one topic.

MY CALENDAR TEMPLATE: AN EXAMPLE

	People Management	Coaching	Project Work	Admin Tasks	Email & Follow-up
	MON 25	TUE 26	WED 27	THU 28	FRI 29
8am					
9am	Catch up on email, update main List, check Capture List, Make Weekly List & Monday Daily List	Power Hours	Meeting block	Meeting block	Power Hours
10am					
11am			Work on big-picture projects, meeting, work, etc.	Low energy/admin tasks	Clear email folders
12pm	Meeting block: 1:1's with my team				
1pm					
2pm	Manager staff meeting	Meeting block for coaching sessions		Meeting block and time for catch-ups	Meeting block
3pm	Low energy				
4pm					Nope
5pm	Make tomorrow's Daily List	Make tomorrow's Daily List and check Capture List	Make tomorrow's Daily List	Make tomorrow's Daily List and check Capture List	
6pm					

Just as it's hard to reach a certain sales revenue target if you haven't set one, it's hard to have an ideal schedule if you haven't mapped one out. Some people continually slot their high-impact tasks over their low-energy times, not knowing why their output isn't what they want. While recognizing these rhythms is the first step, planning *for* them is what radically changes your weeks. To make the switch to this more ideal schedule, it's helpful to do a review of your time and responsibilities to see what you have going on right now.

PRODUCTIVITY PRACTICES

- Print out a blank one-week calendar and try Zero-based Calendaring as a brainstorm activity.
- Sketch in the things that cannot move, your Power Hours and Off-peak Hours, and time to organize and wrap up.
- Try to designate theme days or half days, even a couple of days a week.
- See how you can realistically begin to adapt the realities of your current schedule to this method. It may happen in small steps!

Chapter

6

TIME REVIEW

One executive I worked with had been at Google for almost fifteen years—we'll call her Michele. She had had multiple roles and worked on multiple teams across the world. She came to me for help finding time in her calendar for big-picture visioning and "think time."

The first thing I did was put together a time review with her support team. We listed every commitment she had on a recurring basis, and then sorted her calendar by how much average time per week she was spending on those things. I will never forget her reaction to seeing this all laid out. You could feel her energy shift from shock to excitement as she scanned the list. Her assistant was furiously taking notes as she started making statements like *I totally forgot I was still invited to that! We can cut that out entirely. I can probably stop going to that now; I used to be on that committee for my old team but it's not relevant anymore. Am I really meeting with him for more time than my three other reports combined? Let's cut our meeting from an hour to thirty minutes now that I think of it. That person is no longer relevant to my job so let's start meeting with her quarterly instead of monthly.* Years of accumulated and outdated meetings, commitments, and check-ins were finally being cleaned up and cleared out, much like the exercise of cleaning out a closet or an attic years after the kids have left the nest for good. Suddenly there's all sorts of open space, ready to be redeployed for other endeavors.

In the last chapter you created your ideal calendar layout and a template for your schedule. To understand how to make the most of that template, you have to take a look at the actual allotment of your time *right now*. You may have a general idea based on the "Choosing Priorities" chapter and highlighting activity (for example, how much of your time are you actually spending on the things you care about?), but it's helpful to get the information in a concrete way. It's easy to say *I meet with this person biweekly* or *I spend some time each week on being the room parent at my child's school*, but do you know how many hours you spend doing these things? Do you know how that stacks up to other meetings and commitments you have? It's all vague until you get some data around it and see it in one place. Just like the executive in the above example, there is a whole new clarity to seeing it all laid out, and that's what a time review is for.

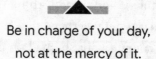

Be in charge of your day,
not at the mercy of it.

WAYS TO REVIEW YOUR CALENDAR

The number and length of meetings are huge concerns for many people when it comes to managing their time, but it's not the way that every person approaches their calendar. Here are a few lenses through which you could view and analyze your calendar, based on what you care most about:

- *Focus versus collaboration*: How much of your time are you spending doing heads-down focus work versus work with others? Is it aligned with what is appropriate for your job?

- *Push versus pull*: What percentage of your calendar is spent on tasks you're being *pulled* into versus things that you're *pushing*, or wanting to get done?
- *Personal time versus work time or Job A versus Job B*: Is your work calendar "leaking" into your personal time? Or vice versa? Especially if you're freelancing, working on different jobs here and there, or working nontraditional hours, it's helpful to know how time is actually adding up and whether the balance is where you want it to be.
- *Responsibilities*: Are you bogged down with hidden commitments that aren't appearing on your calendar but are still sucking up your time? If you have a lot of commitments, but not all of them are represented in meetings, this is a good way to list them all, see how much time you're actually spending on each of them, compare them to one another, and see what you can eliminate.
- *Recurring meetings*: Are you stuck in a rut, still attending meetings that no longer have a purpose? For those who have a say in what meetings they attend, and for how long, this is the easiest way to clean up some of those nonessential things that have been lurking on your calendar forever. Ask yourself with that "zero-based mindset," if I was invited to this meeting today, would I accept and attend every week/month? Much like a streaming subscription, we sign up for a recurring meeting, but until we actively cancel, we're stuck with it forever.

Beware the recurring meeting that
lingers on your calendar even after
it has served its purpose.

To give you an idea of how to collect this data from your calendar, here is an example of a recurring meeting time review (you can find a template for this on my website). You may not have as much authority as the executive in this example in determining what meetings you regularly attend and for how long, but it's a good illustration of how the time review works.

1. Start with putting a list of all the meetings (or commitments) that you attend regularly into a spreadsheet application. You can easily pull this by searching words like *weekly*, *biweekly*, *monthly*, and *quarterly* on your calendar.

2. Add a column in your spreadsheet that indicates how much *time* is actually spent on that meeting or commitment on a monthly basis. Obviously, a two-hour weekly meeting is very different from a half-hour weekly meeting in terms of total time spent or average time per week. Even though they are both listed as "weekly," indexing them to total time or weekly averages can help see where you're spending time.

3. Pick a period of time (I like to do quarterly but annually can work as well) and calculate the total amount of time you're spending on that meeting or commitment in that period.

4. Sort by the total time column to see where you're spending the most time and how the list of activities ranks.

5. Scan the list in descending order, from the highest total minutes per quarter to the lowest, and suggest changes that lighten things up.

	A	B	C	D	E	F	G
1	Person	Est. Frequency	Time /mtg	# of meetings /quarter	# of hours/ quarter	Avg min/ week	Post change check-in: keep or revert back?
2	Leads mtg	Weekly	120	13	1560	120	Keep
3	Gaurik 1:1	Tri-Weekly	25	39	975	75	Keep
4	Steering Committee	Weekly	60	13	780	60	Go if agenda is relevant
5	Naomi 1:1	Weekly	60	13	780	60	Shorten to 30 min
6	Malik 1:1	Twice Weekly	25	26	650	50	Change to once/week
7	LATAM Check-in	Weekly	45	13	585	45	Keep
8	Product Review	Weekly	45	13	585	45	Cancel if we don't have the pre-read
9	GAPP+Velocity	Bi-Weekly	60	7	420	32	Shorten to 45 min

Seeing your calendar broken down like this can be enlightening and empowering. While it takes maybe twenty to thirty minutes to complete this exercise, it will save you *at least* that much time in the long run when you can start making small changes.

Months after meeting with Michele we had a follow-up session. She was glowing. By tweaking the frequency of meetings here and there, trimming others by fifteen minutes, and cutting out some meetings altogether that were no longer important, we had freed up approximately three hours of her time a week. That is so much time when she came to me fighting for every minute of her schedule. The important thing is we cut the things that felt *natural and obvious to be cut out.* She was the one who looked at that list and made the call based on her total time spent. I'd just given her the data and a framework for doing so. She now had three additional hours a week for think time and visioning, almost 150 additional hours a year from this one thirty-minute exercise.

REVISIT YOUR CHANGES

Occasionally when I suggest something like this, people are hesitant to act. *What if I move John from weekly to monthly and then it feels like we're not meeting frequently enough?* Just as we talked about in reference to saying no in Chapter 3, keep in mind that these changes to your schedule do not have to be permanent—try a three-month trial period. If you dropped off that committee but really miss volunteering, sign back up. If you and John are emailing too much now because you don't meet often enough, meet biweekly. If you never test your assumptions, you may never know the right length for recurrence of a meeting.

You can make the changes gradually over time, but what I've heard from many people is that a dramatic change is actually easier. If you have a natural starting point like the beginning of a year, a quarter, a school year, a new job or team, it's a good time to do this sort of refresh. Many executives have told me that they send an email saying, *I'm making some changes to my schedule!* or *Starting in January I'm going to test having biweekly one-on-ones instead of monthly!* That seems to go over better than secretly or quietly making changes that people can take personally. Own the *new you, new schedule, owner of my time* mentality and communicate it! It just might motivate someone else to do the same.

LOOK BACK, LOOK FORWARD

If a full time review feels like too much, a simpler exercise that I use with many of my clients is the *Look Back, Look Forward* weekly reflection. This is based on the principle that sometimes we "power through" our week and never take the time to actually reflect on what was a good use of our time, and what wasn't. Spending a few minutes doing this "pulse check" each week helps when we go to make our plans for the following weeks. If you work with an administrative professional or person who helps with your schedule, doing this exercise together can be especially important so that person can help prioritize your calendar based on your answers to these questions. The more you do this exercise with a person who helps with your schedule, the more they can anticipate where you find value spending your time. Some questions to ask yourself in a Look Back, Look Forward check-in could be (I like to do mine Sunday night when I'm making my Weekly List):

LOOK BACK

- What meetings/activities were a great use of time last week and why?
- What meetings/activities were not a great use of time last week and why?
- Is there anything (meeting/activity) I wish I had spent more time doing last week?
- Is there any meeting/activity that has been rescheduled three or more times? If so, does it really need to happen?

- Is there any meeting/activity on my schedule that I had follow-up items from that I haven't yet captured in my List Funnel somewhere?

LOOK FORWARD

- Is there anything I have on my schedule next week that may not be an excellent use of my time and is there any way to change that?
- Is there anywhere on my schedule next week that Future Me may be low energy or wish I had a break scheduled?
- Is there any meeting/activity on my schedule where I won't be adding value or getting value?

Reflecting on your schedule with these simple questions can help reinforce what *is* a good use of your time, and what *isn't*. The more you do this exercise the more conscious you become week by week of how to spend your time best.

REGULAR TIME REVIEW

It's not necessary to wait for a full review of your calendar to be conscious of how you're spending your time. You can keep this mindset for any single meeting that comes up or even any new commitment. For example, I love to read and I'm in two book clubs that meet once a month. When I moved to a new neighborhood my neighbor asked if I wanted to join their neighborhood book club. My first instinct was *Sure! I love to read!* But then I did a quick time review and figured out if I'm reading 3 books a month, at about 350 pages each, with an average reading speed of about 50 pages an hour, that would end up being 7 hours a week of reading (same analysis could apply by looking at audiobook times). Before joining the new book club I had to seriously ask myself if I could budget an additional few hours a week to complete another book each month (although I've been known to convince my different book clubs to all read the same book at the same time!).

Similarly, if you don't have many recurring meetings or commitments and you just want a quick, simplistic view of how you're spending your time, just pick a date range, like one year or one quarter, and create a pie chart of your top three priorities or your top activities and how much time you're spending on each. If you're an administrative professional managing someone's calendar, this can be powerful data to share with them and help make decisions on their schedule going forward. Some programs like Google Calendar include automatic insights about your time that can even be broken out by the colors you've designated for your events. Any data is good data as you're looking at your time—it's helpful to see where you are now and notice changes if you start to spend more or less time on something.

Sundar Pichai, CEO of Alphabet, does a review of his time every few months. He has a clear sense of the major areas in the company he wants to spend a percentage of his time on, then looks back at his calendar every few months to see whether he spent his time on those things. Any aberrations that come out allow him to step back and think, *What can I do structurally to make sure I get back to how I want to spend my time?* Doing this every few months makes sure he is never too far off course from how his time should be spent.

Think of a time review like going through your closet. It's so refreshing to get rid of things that no longer fit, that are out of style, or that you never wear, and doing so helps override that *endowment effect* of keeping clothes around simply because we *already* own them. Afterward, you can *clearly see* and focus on the clothes you love. Similarly, after a time review you will have room to start reconciling your ideal calendar template from Chapter 5 with your current schedule. Keeping that zero-based mindset ("If I went to the store today would I buy this shirt?"), you can ask of your calendar: *Would I actually add an hour weekly meeting with this person starting today?* If I got the email about joining this volunteer committee today, would I still sign up?

Performed through any of the lenses suggested above—or through one tailored to your own needs—the time review is an invaluable tool for getting rid of things taking up more of your time than they should. Even with time and effort managed this well, sometimes we simply don't do things in the time we have set aside for them. Sometimes we put things off, and when they come up again, we put them off again. Procrastination is something we all succumb to at one time or another. Next we'll discuss easy ways to overcome this bad habit and ways to get ahead of it happening in the first place.

PRODUCTIVITY PRACTICES

- Choose a lens for looking at your calendar with the time review mindset.
- Spend thirty minutes or less reviewing your time to look at things like total time spent or average weekly time.
- Suggest and make changes based on the results, even small ones.
- Check back in after a period of time and ask yourself, *Was it the right decision*? Make changes accordingly.

Chapter

7

PROCRASTINATION AND HOW TO BEAT IT

Even with the best-laid plans, sometimes we add the same thing again and again to our lists, and it keeps being the thing that doesn't happen. We've all seen that one lingering item that keeps dragging its way over from day to day or week to week. Let's say, for example, you want to build a new training module to teach others something you've mastered. You've been carrying it over on your Daily and Weekly Lists and you've blocked time for it, but for whatever reason, it isn't getting done. Sound familiar? Don't be too hard on yourself. It happens to everyone. Here are some tactics and strategies for keeping procrastination from happening.

FUTURE YOU MOOD

As we discussed in Chapter 4, not all time slots are equal. If you're designating 2:30 p.m. to 3:30 p.m. every day to create a new training, but that happens to be your lowest-energy hour of the day, you're setting yourself

The best way to get ahead of procrastination is to make sure you're slotting the right work at the right time.

up either not to do it, or to do less than a great job. If you sit down to do a task and you feel like you're in a boat paddling against the current to do it, it's not the right time. Take a look at items that are lingering on your lists and ask yourself: *When is my* ideal *time or mood to do this? Is it during my Power Hours? Is that when I'm scheduling blocks of time?* Give yourself permission to *not* do something, learn from it, and take note of patterns. Every time I used to plan on doing something that required high energy after my kids went to bed, I never wanted to do it because I wasn't in the mood. I simply never have enough energy points at the end of the evening to do something difficult for my brain. Now I've learned, and no longer schedule things to do in that slot and make sure I have time for them in other parts of my day. Learn to delegate to a Future You who would be excited to do that task.

FITTING IT IN WITH YOUR DAILY THEMES

As we discussed in Chapter 3, it's helpful to have daily themes. With themed days, your brain becomes accustomed to checking in on certain things at certain times and this leaves less room for wondering, *What should I work on today?* Having a themed day or days ensures that you'll check in on those things at least once a week, and gets you in the optimal mindset for doing numerous things on the same topic. If building a new training is something you want to get done, try scheduling it on a day where it feels in step with the theme. If you're trying to build a new training on your *Administrative tasks* day or your *Make outbound sales calls* day, it's more likely to feel difficult to switch to that task. Maybe you have a day themed around whatever you're creating the training about, and after a few meetings on that topic, and answering a few emails on that topic, you'll feel more primed to get the training going.

THE *WHY* OF PROCRASTINATION

To figure out why you're putting something off, we need to first figure out exactly what about the task is causing you to avoid it. Some of the answers could be: *It feels overwhelming. I don't know where to start. I need other pieces of information to get the ball rolling. I know it's going to take a long time.* In the example of the training, maybe it's that you've never built a training before. Timothy A. Pychyl, author of *Solving the Procrastination Puzzle: A Concise Guide to Strategies for Change*, has said there are seven attributes of a task that make us more likely to procrastinate.

1. It's boring
2. It's frustrating
3. It's difficult
4. It's ambiguous
5. It's unstructured
6. It's lacking in intrinsic reward (not fun)
7. It's not meaningful

The more of these attributes that a task has, the more we are likely to mentally resist and avoid it. If you can identify *which* of these attributes a task has, it can help you decide how to move forward better. We can see some examples in the table on the next page.

By nailing down exactly what it is *about* a task that is making you procrastinate, you can reframe the challenge. And tasks can certainly have more than one of these attributes. If doing your taxes is boring, frustrating, *and* not meaningful to you, then you can watch TV while you organize the necessary papers, hire a tax professional, *and* make a

TASK	PROCRASTINATION ATTRIBUTE	HOW TO FLIP IT
Monthly expenses	Boring	Watch a TV show while doing it
Taxes	Frustrating	Talk to a tax professional for help
Write a book	Difficult	Research the first steps as a task itself
Get my team ready for next year	Ambiguous	Write what the three results of ready would be and focus on one to start
Make my yard nicer	Unstructured	Search for pictures of a yard you like and figure out why → implement that thing
Learn to play piano	Lacking intrinsic reward	First learn your favorite song from a video to stoke your enthusiasm
Submit insurance bills for reimbursement	Not meaningful	Make a fun plan of what you'll do with the reimbursement money when it arrives

plan of what you're doing with your tax refund so you're excited about it. Making those three changes can give you a completely different feeling toward the project.

FIVE TACTICS FOR GETTING THROUGH PROCRASTINATION QUICKLY

As much as exploring the *why* of procrastination is essential to overcoming it for the bigger things, you may not always have time to determine the why for every single thing you find yourself putting off. Sometimes the reason for putting something off is just good old-fashioned avoidance! Here are some quick tips for getting through procrastination quickly as it arises.

1. **Swiss cheese to get started.** Sometimes just the *size* of a task is what feels overwhelming, and the hardest part is getting over the hurdle of starting. If my goal is to run every day, that can feel *huge* when the task is to wake up tomorrow at 6:00 a.m. and run three miles. So I think of poking holes in the task, or "Swiss-cheesing" it, until it gets smaller and smaller. You want to find a small enough point that feels like you need less energy points to start, a point where your brain feels okay with it.

   - Running two miles tomorrow morning? *Still feels daunting*
   - Running one mile? *Ehh, still not excited*
   - Waking up at 6:00 a.m. for a walk? *Still would rather sleep in*
   - Wake up tomorrow and put on my sneakers? *That's it? Sure, I can do that!*

   By shrinking the task into something my brain feels good about, I've now lowered the mental hurdle of getting started. Chances are if I set my alarm, wake up, get dressed, and put on sneakers, I'm probably *not* going to go back to bed, fully dressed with my sneakers on. I may even say, *Fine, I'll go on a walk, I already have my shoes on.* Once I'm walking I might jog, and once I'm jogging I might even run three miles. But with three miles as the task, I would have never gotten out of bed.

   In my example about building the training program, this may look like going from *Build a new training* —> *Just open a document and make the title slide.* Making the title slide is fun. It's just one slide! Brainstorming the title is creative and interesting. Once I have it open I might even start drafting some of the other slides.

   On your Daily List or Weekly List you want to write your action in a way that makes you feel excited, or else you will just keep staring at it on the paper. Notice the difference of writing *Make snazzy new training title slide!!* versus *New training.* The first task is doable and is something I know Future Me will be excited to do; the second feels daunting.

2. **Act like your own assistant.** As mentioned before, getting started is the hardest part of some bigger tasks. One way to ease your brain into doing things is to separate the *preparation of doing something* from the *act of doing it,* and to delegate the former to your *assistant self,* which helps break the procrastination barrier.

   For example, I'd been wanting to paint a wooden planter on the center of the table on my sunporch. It was untreated wood and I wanted it to be white. I walked by it three or four times a day—anytime I went out there. It was something I had been meaning to get to, and it bothered me. Why wouldn't I just do it?? Finally, one day when I went into the sunporch with my cup of coffee I thought to myself, *If I was someone's assistant, and I wanted my boss to get this done tomorrow, what would I do to nudge them along gently and make it easier?* So I went out to the garage, got the paint, a paintbrush, and a towel, and just set it all down next to the planter. That's it. Then I went inside. But you'd better believe that the next day when I went out there I thought, *Oh well, the paint is already sitting out here, might as well go ahead and paint it.* It worked like a charm!

   In the training example, I could go ahead and open the slide deck, leave some tabs open with fun relevant clip art and find an example outline from a similar training, then close the computer. The next morning I'd have the way paved for starting that training easily! Now I employ this strategy—channeling my assistant self—for all kinds of tasks at work and at home. If I want to make muffins in the morning, I set out the muffin tin and some ingredients on the counter before I go to bed. Forget the idea of *actually doing it,* which keeps us stuck. Instead, employ your *assistant self* to set up the circumstances under which your boss self (aka Future You) can get it done.

3. **Stop in the middle.** When you are working on a larger, ongoing task that cannot be completed in one sitting, it usually feels right to find a natural stopping point—like the end of an email or the end of a project section. You step away at that point, and let it go until the next time you work on it, when you will start at the beginning of a new section. Ironically, that makes yet *another* starting point that your brain has to get over. It's as if you're starting a large task all over again. Alternatively, stopping in the *middle* of something makes it easier to slide back into what you were doing and start again because you already knew what you were about to do next.

   For example, during my writing blocks for this book, I tried never to stop at the end of a chapter, because for the next writing block I'd have to start with a blank page and a brand-new chapter. Instead I would always stop in the middle of a chapter or at *least* start a new page with a title and outline notes for the next chapter so it was easy to pick it up and get back in the flow. If you're working on large multistep projects, try to stop at a point when your brain already knows the next thing to do. Maybe start drafting that next email to someone, even if you don't have time to finish and send it, because the next time you pick it up you can start right where you left off and get back into the flow of email writing. Similar to the benefit of sending a meeting agenda, or creating a Daily List the night before, you can ruminate on whatever you're in the middle of while you're away, and maybe even come up with a new idea or addition that you hadn't thought of before.

4. **Put a time on it.** Part of convincing yourself to do a task you need to do is wrangling the illusion of how long it actually takes to do it. Have you ever added something to a to-do list week after week, only to realize that the task took so little time that you could have *saved* time just crossing it off, versus the amount of time you spent writing it down again and again? That's one of the reasons I suggest "snack-size" to-do's in my Daily List, because it forces your brain to identify and complete tasks (the ones that take five or

ten minutes) instead of avoiding them. On your Daily List, or any to-do list, you can also write out the time you estimate something will take. For example:

- Draft post for roommate finder website—7 minutes
- Complete sales training—22 minutes
- Read industry article from yesterday—9 minutes

Assigning a specific duration makes it less likely for you to avoid it if you find you do have that amount of time. If you have thirty minutes free, but you don't really want to do the sales training, you have a harder time talking yourself out of it, because you *know* it will in fact be doable during that time. A huge part of productivity is being good at estimating how much time something will take because it helps you slot tasks more effectively. If you're not particularly skilled at that, start to consciously inventory how long things take to sharpen your ability to plan for them.

A good tool for helping you perceive, quantify, and control your time is to determine with certainty how long it takes you to perform some task you do regularly (preferably one you dread), and use that length of time as a comparative unit of measure. Two of my least favorite household tasks are emptying the dishwasher and sweeping the kitchen. I felt like I was always dreading or avoiding those or having the *ugggh* against-the-current feeling every time they needed to be done. So one day I set the timer while I emptied the dishwasher. It took four minutes. *Four minutes.* That's it. I probably spent more than four minutes of the day thinking about how much I didn't want to do it. With this new knowledge I changed my morning routine. I now go downstairs four minutes earlier than I used to. I start by emptying the dishwasher. It adds only four minutes to my morning routine, and I have completely moved past the stress of it by quantifying it. After such a successful mindset shift, I decided to time myself sweeping all of my downstairs floors. It took eight minutes. That's it. Now I try to find pockets of eight minutes throughout the week for that task. My favorite pasta boils for eight minutes—great time to sweep the floor. My husband says he'll be ready to leave the house in about five minutes—which we know will be ten—great time to sweep the floor. It's become a game now. Two tasks that I dreaded and avoided completely were revamped because I quantified the time it took to do them.

5. **Set a meeting to keep yourself accountable.** Usually we are more accountable to others than we are to ourselves. This is why many people look for a workout buddy or join a book club to read more. If we set an arbitrary deadline that only we know about, we're more likely to blow right past it than if someone else is counting on us. If you set up a meeting related to your self-imposed deadline, thereby involving someone else in the process, you can use peer pressure to get things done. For example: If I'm hoping to build that new training I mentioned, *before* I even start building it, I'll set up a meeting invite with someone around the time when I want to be done. *"Hi, Dominic, setting up this thirty-minute slot in a month to get your feedback on my new training! I'll send it to you two days before for your review!"* Have I even started the training at all? Nope. But you'd better believe that now that this meeting is on my calendar, and now that Dominic has accepted it and is looking forward to the meeting, I'm going to be *way* more likely to get it done in time to send it to him. It makes it more *real*. Especially when a task is something you're working on by yourself, find a reason to schedule a meeting or review, or promise someone you'll send it to them. It's one of the best ways to ensure you'll get it done.

Along with the techniques for self-motivation outlined in this chapter, we've learned that determining *why* you're putting off a task is absolutely key to overcoming procrastination. But as important as the *why* in this equation is *when* the work is (or, more to the point, isn't) getting done. While it's helpful to push through some lingering tasks with these procrastination techniques, it's just as important to prioritize downtime and understand why doing nothing sometimes leads to doing more in the long run.

PRODUCTIVITY PRACTICES

- Find a task you've been putting off—ask yourself what daily theme and time of day would be the *best* time to do this and schedule to work on it then.
- Figure out which of the seven procrastination attributes it has, and try to flip it on its head.
- Swiss-cheese the task down to the tiniest task possible, and write that as your to-do list item, including the amount of time estimated to complete it.
- Employ yourself as the assistant to Future You and set all the pieces up to get it done.
- Set a meeting with someone before you've even started a solo task to review and keep yourself accountable.
- Find a repetitive task you dislike and time yourself doing it. Use that knowledge to stop avoiding it and to fit the task into your day.

Chapter

8

HOW DOWNTIME FUELS UPTIME

In the *5 C's of Productivity* discussed in the introduction, the beginning of a new loop or idea starts with *Calm*. When you're calm and you let your brain rest it leads to new ideas. We'll call these calm moments *downtime*. Downtime is the intentional decision to do nothing, rest, or do something that relaxes your brain—and it's *so* important to your overall productivity.

> **To achieve Uptime, you
> must prioritize downtime.**

When I'm speaking to large groups about productivity, I ask them to close their eyes and think of the two places where they get the best ideas. Then I ask them to write those down. I ask them to raise their hand if their list includes one of these locations:

- In the shower? (Roughly half the group)
- On a commute/driving? (One-third to one-half of the group)

- Doing something totally unrelated to work, like cooking or watching your kids play or working out or walking the dog? (Roughly half the group)
- In your tenth back-to-back meeting of the day? (Crickets . . . no hands)
- Knee-deep in your email? (More crickets . . .)

This exercise illustrates that those moments of quiet time, down-time, *me* time, are some of the most important moments in productivity. We used to think of downtime as the opposite of Uptime, but now we know they are both integral to overall performance and well-being. You absolutely must have both in your schedule. Those calm moments of downtime are what lead to the next of the 5 C's, *Create*. By making room in your schedule for *Calm*, you *Create*. Side note: the answers to this exercise also show the importance of having an easily accessible *Capture* list, as discussed in Chapter 3—a list that's available in the shower (voice-activated home devices) or when you're cooking or walking the dog. If you don't capture the loop created in the calm moments, it's nearly impossible to ensure it gets closed or executed.

WHAT IS CREATIVITY, EXACTLY?

Creativity can mean many things, but in the workplace it is very often about building a bridge. It's thinking of two (or more) ideas at the same time that you haven't connected before. And it's virtually impossible to have your active brain turned on (the one that powers through your list, closing loops) at the same time as your quiet, reflective brain (the one that realizes new creative ideas, opening loops). It's just like two people using walkie-talkies: if you want to have a conversation, you can't both talk at the same time. One person has to stop talking for the other person to be heard. You have to stop taking meetings for the day, or stop working on that big project, or stop looking at your email, to be able to generate and pay attention to the ideas that are going to solve

> Space in your calendar translates
> to space in your head. You have to
> prioritize one to get the other.

that problem for you. There is a difference between thinking *about* something and thinking *of* something. And *you* have to create the space for that to happen.

Absolutely no one will ever look at your schedule and think, *Ya know, it looks like she could use some more think/brainstorm time in that schedule. I'm not going to schedule this meeting because she would be better off spending some downtime coming up with ideas than meeting with me,* or *I bet she'd prefer an afternoon walk, so I won't schedule this meeting with her after lunch!* That simply won't happen. You have to make this time for yourself. The best way to create more free time in your calendar? Just take it.

JUSTIFYING THE DOWNTIME

As I mentioned in the introduction, productivity is often measured by output figures and boxes checked. How much did we get done in that day? How much did we check off our list? How many *items* got completed or *meetings* did we have? Just as *busy* is not *important*, neither is *busy* always *productive*.

If you're a manager or leader of a team, I urge you to widen your scope when you look at your employees' output. What they do in a day is not necessarily the only indicator, or even a good indicator, of their overall idea generation and execution. If you're asking a sales employee to make a certain number of phone calls a week—taking up most of their time—do they have any quiet moments to reflect, rethink, and come up with a new way to pitch on any of these sales calls or develop any new strategies for their clients? Having a monthly (instead of weekly) sales quota might encourage more of this type of creativity, leaving the how and when to them for making those calls. Score by the quarter, not the day. January–March might be the new nine-to-five. Similarly, when employees take truly unplugged vacation days throughout the year— where they come back rejuvenated and refreshed—it actually makes them a better employee at the *macro* level of that year (even though they're doing absolutely no work for those days on vacation). Stepping away creates a recharge of energy points to spend at work and in life.

Downtime doesn't have to look like *hours* of time blocked on your schedule or extensive sabbaticals. You don't have to schedule three hours to sit in silence or take six months off. Instead, structure small pockets of intentional downtime, like one or two days of vacation or even just a twenty-minute break in your day. Doing this enables you to process information you've taken in and allows thoughts to gather. A shower is usually less than ten minutes, yet it's continually cited as one of the top places for idea generation. Downtime could be a lunch break *without* your computer or phone, or a walk after work to decompress. Even a workout in the morning before you get to the office counts.

SILENCE IS GOLDEN

Some of these downtime moments could be with others (like a lunch with colleagues), but usually the key to your best creative thinking is being *alone* and *in silence*. You can be doing a task that doesn't require the active part of your brain (knitting, walking, washing dishes, showering), which leaves you with time for your brain to wander. When I had my first

You should have at least one hour of
silent awake time during your day. Even
fifteen minutes here and there adds up.

child, I read *The Montessori Baby: A Parent's Guide to Nurturing Your Baby with Love, Respect, and Understanding,* by Junnifa Uzodike and Simone Davies, which suggests babies should have at least one hour of silent awake time during the day to process all the new senses and things they're experiencing. I tend to think that principle should extend to adults, too. We fill so much of our downtime with noise: podcasts, audiobooks, social media on our phones, following the news. All of those things certainly have their place, but when stacked all together without breaks, that's a lot of noise. Many people are always finding a stimulus that keeps their brain in active/absorption mode, without giving themselves time to let all those new stimuli sink into passive/idea generation mode. *Let your brain be bored.* It's the best thing you can do for your own creativity (and mental health). Rule #2 (of four) in Cal Newport's *Deep Work: Rules for Focused Success in a Distracted World* is Embrace Boredom. A great deal of research, including results of a double-blind study published in 2014, suggests that boring activities lead to increased creativity. Sometimes there is more value in thirty minutes of silence than there is in yet another podcast.

BE BOLD

I like to think of downtime like pour-over coffee. You can always go to the local coffee shop and grab a premade, ready, batch brew, which is the quickest option. The coffee tastes fine and gets the job done. However, you also have the option to order and wait for a drip coffee. Even though it takes a few minutes longer for the water to soak in the grounds, it tastes so delicious and rich and bold and is completely worth the extra time. This coffee is like your idea generation and vision and creativity. Don't choose the grab-and-go mode of having tons of meetings and slurping the batch brew everyday. Put some downtime in your schedule and wait for the rich, bold, robust pour-over ideas to brew. It's worth it.

Think of productivity like a rubber band. You have to pull back to shoot forward at the fastest speed. You can't be going forward at top speed all the time. We all have schedules that vary week to week, with some weeks of more rest or downtime and others that are more intense. I like to call this ebb and flow interval working, which looks like alternative weeks of closing and opening loops. It's a cycle where the down weeks are what give you ideas, energy, and rest for the next big week. If you have a week that's a little lighter, enjoy it!

The process of identifying, protecting, and improving the quality of your downtime is crucial to maintaining the creativity that fuels your work and productivity, and—as we will discuss in the next chapter—the availability of that time has been complicated by the fact that today, many of us don't work in the same place every day, or even on the same type of work one day to the next. In the dynamic, hybrid workspace, finding and conserving downtime is more important than ever.

PRODUCTIVITY PRACTICES

- Ask yourself, when and where do I think of my best ideas? Then look at your schedule. How much of that type of time do you have built into your schedule?
- Think of the output for the people you manage and work with at a macro level. Do they have the freedom to use downtime as productive time and operate effectively?
- Find one hour of silence during your day, even if it's ten minutes here and there. Don't race to turn on a podcast or open your phone every time you have a transition moment or idle moment. Let your brain soak in all the information you process in a day.

PART III

Where to Do It

Chapter

9

LOCATION, LOCATION, LOCATION

When our work schedule was the same every day—commute to the office, work in the same location, with roughly the same hours—our brains didn't have to make many adjustments. It was a recognizable pattern and it made it easy for us to slip into work mode each day. Working from home during the pandemic was a major shift, but after a few weeks it became a new, but consistent, pattern and we adapted to it. Working from home every day required a rewiring of our "normal," but once we grew accustomed to it, our brains and our routines settled down.

Hybrid work—when we're sometimes at home, sometimes in the office, on a schedule that may change from week to week—is a whole new ball game. For the first time ever we are having to train our brains to operate in two (or more) radically different environments, with varying schedules, and even different types of work. Some could argue that hybrid work can feel like having two different jobs. Planning and intention become even more important when you're trying to coordinate schedules with other teammates and decide the best place to do certain work. These tips can help whether you're hybrid, working from home, or working from an office.

OPTIMIZING YOUR CALENDAR FOR CONNECTION AND FOCUS

When the pandemic shifted many of us to working from home, two distinct groups of people emerged: Marathoners and Sprinters.

Some individuals quickly had *more* time than ever—suddenly free from commuting and travel. I call this group Marathoners; they were working from sunup to sundown, in the same spot every day, at the risk of getting burnt-out along the way.

On the other hand, Sprinters had *less* time than ever. Often they had kids at home, some trying to do remote learning, and perhaps a spouse or roommate who was working at home, too. They had to work between kids' naps or meals, and in tiny spurts throughout the day. They were rarely sitting in the same spot to work for more than a few minutes at a time. My advice for these two groups during the pandemic was radically different.

Similarly, with the transition to hybrid work, two other distinct groups of people identified themselves: people who were disappointed because they felt being at home had helped them focus (Homebasers), and people who were enthusiastic about the return to work because they felt more productive out and about and in the office (Outfielders).

With this new insight into our own (and our colleagues') proclivities toward home or office work, we can maximize our productivity by

Recognizing *where* we focus best enables
us to develop new routines and new
locales for doing our best work.

fine-tuning our schedules and personal workspaces along the lines suggested by this chart:

Homebaser (focus-better-at-home person)	Outfielder (focus-better-at-work person)
• Schedule large blocks of time on home days that are uninterrupted • Push any meeting (even virtual) to a day in the office if possible • Set up home office to minimize distractions (no phone, headphones, closed door, extra monitor, etc.) • Consider a schedule at home that optimizes your focus (mid day workout, early morning start, late break for lunch to keep morning momentum) • Plan that days at the office will be more "scattered" and have a list of small "snack- size" to-do's that day that can be accomplished in small bursts of focus time • Don't waste days at home on small menial tasks or quick emails that can wait until your next day in the office • Prioritize big projects that need heads-down focus • If you have the ability to choose, choose to go into the office on days that are already full of meetings, even virtual	• Schedule large blocks of time in the office that are focus oriented and uninterrupted • Push meeting requests when possible to your days at home (even if meeting could be in person in the office, okay to take it virtually from home for focus's sake) • Set up your office to minimize distractions: large headphones or a small touch lamp on your desk to indicate focus to colleagues, extra monitor(s), book an office or conference room if necessary • Plan that days at home will be more "scattered" and have a list of small snack-size to-do's those days that can be accomplished in small bursts of focus time • Don't waste days in the office on small menial tasks or quick emails that can wait until your next day at home; prioritize big projects that need heads down focus • If you have the ability to choose, choose to go into the office on days that are clear of meetings and have more focus time

ADJUST TO YOUR CIRCUMSTANCES

Not all of us are working hybrid. Some are fully at home and some are fully back in the office. In some cases, those who love to work in an office (still Outfielders!) are in a fully remote job and now find themselves at home full-time. My husband (a true Outfielder) recently became remote and found that he had a harder time focusing at home. He didn't have the option to go into an office but started to find ways to get *out* nonetheless. Whether it's working at a coffee shop, at a coworking center, or even at the library, he's found ways to mimic an office situation. He's created rhythms for himself that are similar to office work: he gets up, gets dressed in professional clothes, and heads to a location to work for the day, and that works for him to feel his most productive.

Similarly, if you're a Homebaser who has to go back into an office full-time, you may want to carry with you the things you love about working from home. If it's the ability to focus without chatter, consider headphones or asking for an office or booking a conference room so you can get focus work done. If it's the flexibility of schedule, talk to your manager about working with your natural rhythms, even if that means coming in at a different time every day. No matter what your situation, if you first identify yourself as a Homebaser or Outfielder, it can help you adjust your schedule to make the most of your working situation.

COLLABORATION IN THE HYBRID WORKPLACE

While a hybrid schedule can mean splitting your time between multiple locations as an individual worker, it can also mean collaborating with a mix of colleagues and locales (remote, hybrid, in person, virtual).

This presents new challenges to working productively and collaboratively as a team. Over the course of my coaching I've seen leaders and teams adopt the practices below to help facilitate more seamless collaboration, no matter where and how their team is working:

1. **Communicate where you are.** This one seems obvious, but was consistently coming up when I worked with teams in the early days of hybrid work. People were working from different offices some days, from home other days, without making it abundantly clear on their calendars where they were. It made scheduling with teammates

difficult, especially when tons of employees were having to play a workplace version of *Where's Waldo?*, figuring out who was where and on what days. That's why I advocate taking time to mark your calendar with your location, and keep it updated. Block time for personal commitments, travel time between buildings, and the other little things that make you briefly unlocatable. Comb through and update your calendar each week as thoroughly as you would look through a bank account statement scanning for discrepancies.

2. **Set rules of engagement.** Just as multiple inefficiencies can scale across an organization and create problems, setting core rules that are followed by a whole team or organization can scale positively and make communications run smoothly. Below are some examples of rules of engagement I've seen work well.

As a team:
- We schedule all Asia/US meetings on Tuesday night/ Wednesday morning when possible.
- We have no meeting Fridays to make room for heads-down work.
- We all are in the office on Wednesdays.
- We send chats only when urgent or regarding a same-day request—otherwise we email.
- We make all calendar events modifiable by all parties so they can be easily moved and changed without additional emails.
- We don't email on weekends.

3. **Level the playing field.** Another striking aspect of working from home is the fact that everyone is reduced to the same-size square on a screen. It equalizes us in group meetings and chats, encouraging some to speak up when they maybe wouldn't have sitting at a large conference room table. Trying to keep this consistency can be

helpful now that you likely have people in the office, people on their computers, and people at home or other remote locations. Many virtual meeting platforms offer the ability for everyone to join the comment box or virtual whiteboard, even if they're physically present in the conference room. If your team loves the hand-raising function in virtual-only meetings, make sure to encourage hand raising even in person. Intentionally include those who are not in the main room by asking them directly, *Josh, what do you think?*

4. **Create a separate space for social engagement.** Like many teams during the pandemic, my team really missed social connection with our colleagues. We had lots of one-off meetings with each other throughout the week and found that it was inefficient to try to fit social time into each one of these meetings. I'd meet with Beth and catch her up about my weekend. Later I'd have a meeting with Beth and Michelle and tell Michelle about my weekend, which Beth had already heard. Before I knew it each meeting was filled with repetitive stories and catch-ups that were encroaching on much-needed meeting time.

   With this in mind, our teammate Vivian created a weekly *social-only* meeting. It was a standing half hour on Wednesday. It relieved the pressure of each of us having to catch all the others up in various forums on what was going on in our lives, the weekend, and elsewhere. We could use other meetings for business and even shorten them to ten or fifteen minutes, knowing that we had time set aside to connect midweek.

   However, nothing falls flatter than a virtual social catch-up where people are instructed to just chat (and of course any meeting I'm part of has to have an agenda!), so we even made a weekly agenda to keep it fun and interesting. After a quick round-robin update about how we were doing personally, each week had a different theme. Some examples included:

   • Bring and introduce your pet day

- *MTV Cribs*–style tour of a favorite room of your house
- Self-care September: Each week had a different focus, our best tips for mental, physical, spiritual, and emotional health
- Favorite store-brand items month: Each week we discussed a different retailer, Trader Joe's, Costco, Target, and Aldi
- Teach a skill you know to others month: Each week was led by a different person, skilled in things like sewing, wreath making, and cocktail mixing
- Easy recipe day: Everybody brings and shares a recipe that takes thirty minutes or less to make
- Book in a minute: Summarize your favorite nonfiction book and what it taught you in minute, round-robin style

This meeting was so popular and helpful that we continue to hold it even though many of us do see each other in person now. The weekly touch-base ensured that those of us working virtually are caught up and feel included, alleviated the need for socializing in every meeting, and led to other spontaneous collaboration and work-related ideas. Thirty minutes of weekly social interaction adds up to far less time than trying to socialize for the first ten minutes of every meeting throughout a week.

5. **Embrace asynchronicity.** The fact that we are all no longer in the same place, at the same time, may also require you to rethink workflows. Using tools like collaborative documents and chats; scheduling emails to send during the recipient's work hours appropriate to their time zone; giving two options for an all-team meeting so it can be attended by individuals in different time zones; moving a brainstorm to a virtual whiteboard where people can add to it on their own time versus chatting at the watercooler—all of these are examples of ways to embrace the new way of work.

Remember that hybrid—in all senses—really is a *different* way of working. In the spirit of zero-based thinking, I used to tell my clients:

Imagine you just got let go from your current role. Now congrats! You just got hired again—for the same position, except it's working partially from home, and your team is spread out and working hybrid. With this new job mindset, think about how you can go into the role and approach it with a fresh perspective. Hybrid is a different way of working and should be treated that way.

Hybrid work is here to stay for many of us and the strategies and techniques outlined here will help you adapt and thrive in this context. No matter how well we have planned and organized, however, there is an important part of us—our brain—that may not adapt so easily to such change and fluidity. In the next chapter we'll discuss ways to ease that adjustment as well.

PRODUCTIVITY PRACTICES

- Analyze your work habits and ask yourself where you focus best. Use the chart in this chapter to adjust your calendar and workspace accordingly.
- Ask your team to do the same self-assessment. Using their responses (and your own observations), find rules of engagement for meetings and communication for your team to make the most of hybrid work schedules.
- Decide where and how social collaboration will happen within your team. Foster it with a weekly virtual meeting or weekly social engagements when everyone is in the office.

Chapter

10

HOT SPOTS AND NOT SPOTS

When I put my one-year-old son in the high chair, why does he start drooling even before I've started to prepare the food? I'd love to think it's because I'm such an *amazing* chef, but the reality is that his brain has correctly learned to associate *high chair* with *food*, and that brain connection has triggered a consistent physical change with his salivary glands.

Similarly, why do you hear of many authors who wrote their entire book sitting in the same spot? Or why do some people listen to the same piece of classical music to focus, or to fall asleep? Or, conversely, why did so many of us have difficulty switching our work to a home office at the beginning of the pandemic? It's all because of the same thing: *state dependency*.

State dependency refers to the fact that our brains take in so much more than just *what* we're doing. They have context clues like where we are, what we smell, what we hear—information stored in our brain that we then associate with *what* we were thinking about or doing.

This works for memory, too. In 1975, two groups of deep-sea divers were asked to memorize a random list of thirty-six two- and three-syllable words. One group memorized on land, one underwater. Before being asked to recall the words, half the underwater group was put on land, and half the land group underwater. Those recalling in the same setting as that in which they'd learned the words had a far higher rate of accuracy.

HOT SPOTS

When we recognize that our brain is associating certain places with certain tasks, we can manipulate that tendency to our advantage. Ever wonder why it took no time at all to get into the mood of work when you were going into the office every day? It's because so many other conditions were lined up before you even opened your computer: your commute, your desk, your office, your chattering cubemates, your favorite coffee mug. All of these were cues that your brain was consistently associating with work *every single day*. They were "greasing the wheel" before you even sat at your desk. No wonder it was easy for your brain to start thinking about work at work, and no wonder it was hard for many of us to slip into work mode at home when we had none of those cues available.

You can use this human inclination to your advantage by creating physical *hot spots* for certain types of work. This can be done whether you have multiple locations for hybrid work, or even if you work from the same location every day, like the home or office.

This *task:location* association could look like:

- I always do my expenses at the big comfy window chair in my office.

Choosing specific locations for specific
tasks helps you ease into them.

- I always read product design documents at a coffee shop near my house on work-from-home days.
- I always start the day reading industry news on my phone on the front porch.
- I always respond to emails first thing in the morning with my cup of coffee at my desk.
- I always code on my home office days with my double monitors.
- I do all of my content writing at the office with my door closed.

You want to pair these things with your already curated calendar template from Chapter 5, along with your decision on what types of tasks you need to do at home or the office based on your focus preferences. Once you have the general idea of your daily themes, where you'll be, and what you'll be focusing on generally, you can get down to the nitty-gritty of where you'll sit to do it. Of course it doesn't have to be every single time, but the more consistent you are, the easier it becomes for your brain to slip into focus mode for that particular task in that particular location.

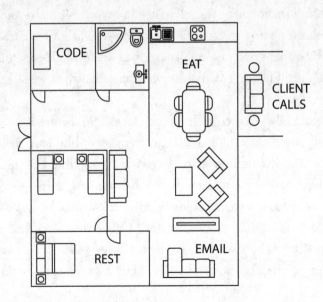

NOT SPOTS

If I put my son into his high chair every once in a while just to read him books or to play with toys, then lifted him out without giving him food, his brain would stop making that easy food association. He'd now think, *Who knows why I'm in the high chair? Could be anything!* and the direct connection to food for that location would be lost. That's why it's important to preserve certain locations for certain activities and not mix them.

Equally as important as having your *hot spots* is creating your *not spots* to help your brain *not* think about certain things when you're in certain places. This will preserve your emotional well-being and stimulate your ability to relax.

When so many of us were forced to work from home, it could feel like we were living at work all the time. During the pandemic, I urged my clients to treat work like any other guest in their home. If you had your in-laws staying with you, maybe a little uninvited or a few days too long, how would you handle that? You would create boundaries; you would give them their own space. You would *not* hang out with them every single night until the moment you fell asleep or invite them into your bedroom every morning first thing at 6:00 a.m. However, that's what we're doing with our work by opening email as soon as we open our eyes, and working right up until bedtime, which is what happens when we sleep with our phones next to us.

My dad has worked from home since 1996, before it was common to do so. My entire childhood, I can't remember him ever bringing work into our family common space. Recently I asked him how he kept such great boundaries. He told me that, when he first started working from home, he had no other option. Wi-Fi wasn't available, so he had to be plugged into an ethernet outlet and, before that, only had a desktop computer. Now he can bring his laptop other places around the house, like out by the pool to send emails, but once he had established our living room and kitchen area as the place he visited with his family and *never* worked, they stayed his safe-from-work places forever (his *"not spots"*).

When my husband and I first moved into our new house with our children, we had this awkward side area of our primary bedroom that I had no idea what to do with. It wasn't big enough to be a total sitting area but not small enough to just put a table. Eventually we moved a chair-and-a-half there along with some blankets, a bookshelf, and a coffee machine. It quickly became known by my kids as the "cozy corner."

The cozy corner is where I finish a cup of coffee before my kids wake up (which is, in my opinion, the golden key to parenting). It's where I read books and magazines or meditate. It's where my daughter meets me in the morning when she wakes up, bringing a book of her own. There's no clock in the cozy corner (I set alarms with my phone across the room if I need to know when it's time to go do something). I often catch myself wanting to bring my laptop there to finish a few emails, or to bring my phone to scroll on social media, but I resist, because never once in that chair has my brain actively thought about work, stress, or anything but relaxation. I associate that corner 100 percent with being cozy, my kids, reading, and relaxing. Why would I ruin that? It's so easy for me to unwind in that corner, and that is why I love it.

You need those safe spaces in your life and, unfortunately, having devices that are easily accessible anywhere has endangered those sanctuaries. So it's something you have to be intentional about, to design for. Find a place or two in your life—a physical spot, at a regular time of day—where all you do is . . . *relax*. Maybe it's on your commute where you never take phone calls or read emails and only listen to an audiobook or music (or silence!). Maybe it's your living room or bedroom. Never let your stressful stuff seep in there, and watch how much easier it is to relax and unplug in those spots. Even if you've previously blurred the lines of locations, you can always start over, retraining your brain to expect nothing but relaxation in these specific spots.

CREATE CONSISTENCY

As we discussed in Chapter 9, having a hybrid work schedule can sometimes feel like having different jobs in different places. If your job includes traveling to different locations every week, it can be hard to get into a routine with hot spots and set schedules. No matter where you're working, you can help your brain with these transitions by finding a few things that you do every single weekday (no matter where you're working).

For example, if you commute from 8:15 a.m. to 9:00 a.m. on the days you go into the office, and listen to an audiobook on the way, go on a walk and listen to your book during the same time period on days when you work from home. If you always take a walk at home after lunch, do it at work, too. Always get an afternoon coffee at the office? Make yourself a latte at home. Usually get a workout every morning at home? Try to do the same at the hotel when you're traveling. These types of signals help you keep your flow and make it a *consistent* workday no matter where you are. They set the stage for the day to be productive and about work.

Similar to creating not spots, you can also create a routine you follow only on *nonworkdays* to trigger your brain into relaxing and thinking: fun. Maybe it's that you make pancakes every Saturday morning, or you take the time to use your cappuccino machine on the weekends. If you have children, they'll *love* fun weekend traditions that indicate something is different about this day, as opposed to other school/weekdays.

STAY IN THE FLOW, WHEREVER YOU GO

When it comes to hybrid work, the techniques I describe in this book—theming your days, grouping your meetings, and planning intentionally in a Daily List—become even more important. Take a good look at your calendar template from Chapter 5 and ask yourself:

Does it make sense with the hybrid lens?

Do I have a theme for a certain day that would be better if I was in the office that day, or with more of my colleagues?

Should I shift my commute time based on what I know about my peak hours (that is, do some focus work from 7:00 a.m. to 9:00 a.m. at home, *then* drive in to work)?

Once you know what types of work you like to do where, in what specific spots, this starts to drive your Weekly and Daily Lists a little more precisely. Bouncing around from place to place each week or working with colleagues in multiple locations makes it even more important to be certain about these items.

Think of hot spots, not spots, grouping, and planning ahead as tools to help your brain adapt to the most successful hybrid work schedule. Having the knowledge of where and how you work best, coupled with the intention of what you do where, can set you up for success regardless of your location or schedule.

PRODUCTIVITY PRACTICES

- Choose *hot spots* for a few of your top tasks. For instance, *I always answer client emails in the chair at my office.* Start training your brain to associate those spots with those tasks.
- Choose *not spots*: places where you never actively work. Start using those spots for relaxation only.
- Create workday consistency. Come up with a few routines you always do no matter where you're working that day.
- Use the *hybrid lens* to take a look at your schedule, based on what days you have to be where and what themes and groupings you have for your day. Does it make sense? Does it flow with your energy? Adjust accordingly.

PART IV

How
to Do
It Well

Chapter

11

THE BALANCE OF BOUNDARIES

You've identified the tasks that are most important (*what*). You've identified your peak times to get those things done (*when*). You know how to fit those into your new hybrid locations and specific spots (*where*). But now that you've set all that up, the last piece is making sure you execute *excellently* within those new parameters you've defined. This is where people typically think of efficiency when it relates to productivity. How do I actually get the things done in the *best way possible?*

A huge part of that starts with how you work with others. No one operates in a bubble, so you need a plan for how your priorities and time preferences will fit into working with others. Many people think that you have to choose between being "one of those people" (one who asks to see the agenda, doesn't attend every meeting they're invited to, says no to requests or new projects) *or* being one who has social capital and is viewed as friendly, accessible, and well respected. You don't have to choose! You can be both. You can be protective of your time and intentional about how you spend it, but do it in a friendly way that promotes collaboration and fosters mutual respect.

Once I ran into an old colleague and friend, Mark, in one of our

New York offices, when we were both visiting. He said, "*Oh hi! It's so great to see you! I'd love to catch up soon so I'll add time to your calendar and of course I'll be sure to send over an agenda beforehand.*"

Right then and there I thought: *I've done it!* The fact that Mark still wanted to catch up with me, enjoyed working with me, and was keeping in touch years after we were on the same team showed that I was friendly enough to be a good person to work with. His endorsement of me was part of why I had previously gotten promoted. But he *also* knew my working style and high standard for time well spent. I built "my brand" as someone who wouldn't accept meetings if there wasn't an agenda: that's exactly the brand I wanted! I had successfully set that as a boundary.

You may be coming up with reasons why you can't make or keep boundaries, such as: *I own my own business, I have to be available, I just started my job on the "bottom of the ladder,"* or *I have to take what I can get.* While some of these things may be true, think of setting boundaries very slowly, one step at a time. I worked with a client who took a new job and her predecessor let her know that he had worked nights, weekends, and vacations in the role. She wasn't comfortable with this even though it was the standard that had been set before her. It would have been polarizing for her to jump into her new role with a radically different working style, so we came up with a gradual boundary approach. As she was first getting ramped up in her new role, she did respond to emails and pings outside her working hours. After a few weeks in, she started waiting an hour to respond to those and telling those she worked with that she was having dinner with her family and would respond after that dinner. Slowly that worked into responding to those things immediately the next morning, during her working hours. She took her first vacation checking emails once a day, but that slowly moved to one to two times during the week she was out. After about a year her colleagues both respected and enjoyed working with her, but she had gradually shifted the expectations of her role to be something that worked with *her* individual boundaries. The following year she was promoted and that was likely due to the time and energy she was putting into her role *and* the positive benefits of being rested and unplugged during her downtime.

Think about someone you know who has set a boundary with you—you likely respect them more *because* of it. For example, my favorite photographer told me nicely that she takes family pictures only on Tuesdays and Thursdays, so she can edit on Wednesdays and shoot weddings on the weekend. Ideally I would like to have her come take pictures on the weekend but I also respect that she's set this schedule up for herself. The confidence (and friendliness) she has about this shows me that she's professional and intentional about her time. I am certainly still going to hire her if she takes good pictures and I bet her pictures would be better than those from someone who will shoot pictures at any time slot requested on any day. This photographer's boundaries have set her up to be more balanced and refreshed for editing—the work she produces will be better as a result and she will be a better photographer, and attract more clients who are happy to adhere to her schedule.

A lot of my coaching focuses on how to walk this line, which can be especially challenging for people in a new role or for people trying to lighten up their schedules. How do I stay collaborative, approachable, and available to my teams and colleagues while preventing myself from living in *their* world, with their to-do list taking priority over mine? It's a delicate balance but it can certainly be achieved.

WHAT ARE YOUR THREE BOUNDARIES?

In addition to asking, *What are your top three priorities?* one of the first questions I ask when I begin working with a client is, *What are three boundaries you've set for yourself?* Many times the reaction to that question shows immediately how much thought has been put into this. Either someone has defined boundaries or they've never thought about it before. Some examples of boundaries from others I've seen that are realistic and work really well:

- I take all meetings between 8:00 a.m. and 4:00 p.m.
- I leave at 5:00 p.m. every day to pick up my kids.
- I walk my dog at lunch every day.
- I take meetings Monday–Thursday and schedule focus work on Friday.
- I do networking meetings one week of the quarter.

Having boundaries doesn't mean that they are *never, ever* crossed but it should mean that you're sticking to them about 80 percent of the time or more. Even sticking to them *most of the time* makes a huge difference. Just like we discussed in Chapter 4, implementing this change *to any degree* will yield a positive effect. The practice of simply listing and defining your boundaries helps you reflect on what matters most to you and highlights what will give you the most ROI on your time or energy. Boundaries are not the same for everyone, so defining them for yourself is hugely important.

ON THE POSITIVE SIDE

I taught barre workout classes for ten years and one thing we were trained on is to always use positive language on the microphone. Telling someone *"Stop bending your knee"* requires so much more thinking and deliberation on their part than just telling them *"Straighten your leg."* Using positive language gives your brain one single thing to focus on, what you *should* do. I've seen this work in countless ways from my coaching to workplace communications and even parenting (*"Don't yell!"* vs. *"Quiet please!"*).

The bridge between boundaries and approachability is the right communication. The best way to communicate boundaries is to frame from the positive. You'll notice in all the above examples the boundary is highlighting what you *do* do versus what you *don't* do. Consider framing your boundaries this way anytime you communicate them:

NEGATIVE FRAMING OF BOUNDARY	POSITIVE FRAMING OF BOUNDARY
I don't take meetings on Friday.	I take meetings Monday–Thursday.
We don't watch TV on the weekdays.	We watch TV on Saturdays and Sundays.
I don't instant message outside my work hours.	I'm available by messaging between 7:00 a.m. and 5:00 p.m.
I can't do a career chat this week.	I do career chats on the third Thursday of the month.
I don't do family portraits on the weekend.	I'm available Tuesdays or Thursdays for family portraits.
I leave work every day at 5:00 p.m.	I'm available to meet before 5:00 p.m.
I'm not taking any new clients right now.	I'm taking new clients starting in May.
I don't review contracts in less than twenty-four hours.	I address all contracts within forty-eight hours.
I don't have time during the week to meet about this topic.	I have office hours every Friday where I can meet on this topic.

You can see how the same exact boundary sounds and feels a lot better when communicated from the positive point of view. It keeps the receiver of the boundary focused on what you *can* and will do versus what is off-limits.

THE YOU-SER MANUAL

Once you have your boundaries set and framed using positive language, it's best to communicate them up front to avoid having to repeat

Boundaries are nothing if
not advertised widely.

them *as* a situation comes up. The best way to advertise them widely is to
list them wherever you can, for example, on a company profile page, in your
email signature, or anywhere that's easily accessible to people you work
with. You can also repeat your boundaries to others frequently within
your workflow. I decline vague calendar invites often with the note that
says, "I only attend meetings with an agenda ☺!" (I usually add the smiley
just to reconfirm the friendliness, but that can be a style decision.)

A couple of Google leaders, including Urs Hölzle, SVP of Engineering, have popularized a sort of "user manual" or "how to work with me
guide." Urs explains his working style, his preferences for meetings, and
how he likes to be asked for decisions. He has it published as a link on
his company profile page and updated at all times for others to see. This
is a great way to take the guesswork out of working with others. You can
clearly show when and how you prefer to communicate (email, instant
messages, meeting, or phone call), as well as your current priorities and
boundaries.

One thing I talk about often with my clients is that when things get
intense, the "pressure" will hit you somewhere. If people are emailing you
but you're behind on email, they will add time to your calendar. If you
don't have a spot on your calendar, they will message you to get answers
or decisions. If you clearly define your communication preferences (let's
say you're not great at checking email and you'd much rather start with a
quick five-minute sync), then you can save yourself the "pressure spread"
by stating this in the first place! I stay on top of my email easily but find
myself overwhelmed when my calendar is overbooked, so I list my first
line of communication preference as email. Work style and communication preference can be a great starting point and something you post
publicly or share with your teammates.

If this is not a common practice where you work, start small by sharing boundaries or work style preferences with just your immediate team or
manager. During a quarterly off-site or team meeting, have some discussions around what would make your group work better together, and what
makes you work better as an individual. Generate a list of preferences for

members of your team, like: *Kyle prefers to be sent an email before scheduling anything on calendar!* Or *Ma'ayan likes to have thirty-minute breaks between her meetings if possible!* Suggest displaying these boundaries or preferences somewhere easy for others to see. Check in after a few weeks and see how communication and workflow have improved.

MORE BANG FOR YOUR ENERGY BUCKS

While it's important to make your boundaries realistic, it's equally important to make it clear that you're approachable, and available for quality face time and collaboration within those boundaries. Inefficiencies can often result from our efforts to make ourselves available. We can do more with less of our time and spend fewer energy points for more collaborative time.

1. **Office hours:** If you find yourself with a lot of meetings that aren't part of your regular cadence, normal working group, or top priorities, consider having weekly office hours. It should be for things that are more of the *pull* category (when you're being asked something or being pulled into something). Schedule it for your lower-energy times. If people want to meet with you who are outside of your regular priorities—say, someone who wants career advice from you—they'll likely make the office hours time slot work. Do very short time slots to start (maybe ten minutes). Create office hours rules, like that you must receive any materials they want reviewed by a night or two beforehand, or that any relevant decision maker needs to be included in the meeting. Let people know when they feel like they need your time that you have office hours available anytime they want to chat. Merely establishing office hours makes the point that you're available, whether people end up using that time or not, just like the college professor example from Chapter 1.
2. **Group similar meetings:** Another way to keep your boundaries is to group similar recurring meetings together. One executive I

worked with realized that she held separate meetings with different engineering groups, but they all ended up having the same questions. So for her, it was the same meeting three times a week, and for all of the engineers, an important meeting to get their questions answered. We brainstormed ways to streamline these meetings and ultimately decided to combine the three meetings into one engineering Q&A, where all three groups could ask questions. After this change, we found that many of the engineers had the same questions and that asking them in a larger group allowed for even greater information sharing and brainstorming, ultimately benefiting all of the teams involved and freeing up time on her calendar. You can apply this same lens to your calendar. If you have a large number of one-on-ones, see if there are ways to consolidate them into two-on-ones, four-on-ones, or even one-to-manys. Perhaps you find that you're meeting twice a week with a similar group of people, with the exception of one or two attendees. In this case, could you make it one meeting, extend it by fifteen minutes, and have the one or two extra people show up just for the last part? Be strategic in how you can make the most of your own time.

3. **Embrace shorter meeting times:** Sometimes you need to check in with people, but you don't always need to check in for as long as you think. Be okay with having a fifteen-minute check-in. Be open to shortening standing meeting times, which will require presenters to be more succinct. Scarcity breeds innovation and making your meeting times short is a perfect example. One of my favorite activities that's common at Google is *Lightning Talks*, where presenters have one slide and three minutes to teach the audience something, get buy-in for their idea, practice a sales pitch, or give an update on a project. The presentations are automatically timed so that after three minutes, the next slide appears, and you're "kicked off" the stage. The audience is instructed to clap loudly when they see the next slide so presenters know it's time for them to go. It's amazing how much is communicated when the presenter knows

ahead of time that they have only three minutes to make an impact. They "trim the fat" from their presentations; they make their one slide visually stimulating and compact, including only the most important elements. They have one chance to make an impact, and they make the most of it. Not to mention the audience is highly engaged because the information is succinct and they aren't being asked to listen to anything extraneous. It's similar to the TV-ad style that *Sesame Street* adopted at its inception (with "commercials" promoting numbers and letters). Adults and children alike find it easier to consume short, concentrated bytes of information rather than long, overly complicated material. (More on how to make shorter meetings in Chapter 13.)

4. **"While I do this":** Another way to make more of less time is, when possible, to do meetings or tasks simultaneously with others (that don't distract you). If you normally take a walk midday, make it a walking meeting and catch up with someone. If you need to eat lunch anyway, ask someone who has been requesting to do a check-in to eat lunch with you. If you already have to wait in the car during soccer practice, can you take a call then? You should always be thinking about the things you *already* need to do and how you can slot in things you also should do with them.

I worked with an executive who had just joined Google and was stepping into a new role. He managed global teams spanning continents, time zones, and different areas of the business. A time review showed us that he was spending a large amount of his time trying to connect with team members spread out all over the world. He had kept team meetings that had already been in place and also added new ones to his calendar in order to get to know everyone. He felt stretched thin, and even though his days were booked, he wasn't able to attend to his top priorities.

After taking a closer look at his schedule, we made the following changes:

- Instead of a "Noogler" (new Googler) meeting with each person in his organization, we grouped them into a quarterly Noogler/Dave lunch, effectively turning nine thirty-minute, one-on-one meetings (four and a half hours) into a single hourlong meal. Most of the Nooglers' questions and discussions were similar anyway, and as a bonus, they got to meet all the other new people in the organization.
- Instead of having one-on-one meetings all over his calendar from various members of his organization, we established two days at the beginning of the quarter where individuals could sign up for fifteen-minute slots to meet with him, narrowing his focus for just those two days, and freeing up time the rest of those weeks.
- We changed his weekly team meeting from two hours to forty-five minutes. While this feels like an aggressive jump, we wanted to radically change the feel of the meeting so people treated it like it was something different. He'd felt like the time was usually filled with things that could be discussed in other forums, and he already had individual weekly check-ins with each person on his team. The new meeting had more pre-reads and shorter presentation slots, and we agreed on a two-month test to see how it went.
- We decided to change his travel schedule to one location per quarter, and did a longer all-team meeting during each visit, instead of monthly all-team meetings for each country (more impactful because it was in person and everyone made sure to prioritize it).
- We set up office hours each Friday for any meetings unrelated to his core work.

When I met with him again a few months later, the change was *radical*. His team still felt like they were getting appropriate face time with him (he took an anonymous team-wide survey and responses were positive). By strategically moving some of his meetings to in person, he actually saw team members even more and he still met every new person who joined his organization within the first few months of their arrival. Most importantly, he was a better leader. He had more time in his schedule for things he wanted to push forward for his team. He was operating effectively—all because of these "more bang for your energy bucks" scheduling changes we had made.

SAYING NO IS EASIER WITH BOUNDARIES IN PLACE

No discussion of the importance of setting boundaries would be complete without acknowledging that sometimes you'll just plain be saying *No.* And that's okay. Chapter 2 outlines some great tactics to use when you need the language to say, *That doesn't work for me.*

The great thing about setting clear and deliberately communicated boundaries is that you have to say no much less often. By telling people up front that I keep Friday mornings free for focus time and blocking that on my calendar, I've already eliminated the need to decline any meeting on Friday. No one will schedule it there. By stating in my user manual that I prefer only to use instant messaging for urgent matters, I almost never get those messages that I have to ignore or redirect, and instead see requests funnel through my email, exactly where I prefer them.

It's helpful to reference your boundaries anytime something crosses one of them, so it's clear why you're saying no, and it's less likely to happen again. You can say, "As a reminder I'm only available for meetings before 7:00 p.m. so I won't be at this one," or "As you can see in my user manual (link) I prefer to start discussions over email before having a meeting so please send over your thoughts and I'll respond and see if we need to set up time!! Thank you!"

Having boundaries in place makes saying no less personal. It's not that I'm saying no to *this specific* meeting, it's that I'm saying no to any meeting after 7:00 p.m. It's not that I'm ignoring *your* message outside of work hours, it's that I specifically said since the beginning of my time working here that I answer chats during my working hours, 8:00 a.m.–5:00 p.m. Boundaries give structure, which helps support working relationships and your own mental clarity.

Of course, there is some flexibility that comes with these boundaries (if a senior manager asks to meet with you at a time you'd prefer not to meet, you would likely flex your schedule to accommodate), and there will always be things out of your control with your schedule. The point is to have some boundaries and preferences for the things you *can* control. If someone who views you as a mentor asks you to meet, you *do* have the flexibility to ask them to get lunch when you already planned to take a break and eat, versus taking up another thirty-minute slot on your schedule. Similar to the calendar template we discuss in Chapter 5, the goal is to focus on anything you *can* control in your schedule and make the most of it. All companies and cultures are different, so if boundaries and preferences aren't regularly practiced, introducing some of these concepts will be a gradual process. You now have the language and tools to begin these sorts of conversations.

The clear and thoughtful setting of boundaries is crucial to protecting our time, energy, attention, and brainpower. Straightforward boundaries allow our colleagues to collaborate more successfully with us, and enable us to work as effectively and creatively as possible. How we plan for the time and space protected by those boundaries isn't merely a matter of instituting the list and calendar practices and techniques we've discussed in previous chapters. Really good planning has a benefit all its own.

PRODUCTIVITY PRACTICES

- What are three boundaries you have for yourself? State them in the positive.
- Write a short *how to work with me* you-ser manual and share it widely or even just with your teammates and colleagues.
- Look at your calendar and figure out how to get more for your energy points: combine, shorten, or rearrange meetings where possible.
- When saying no, reference your boundaries or user manual to get others in the habit of knowing what they are.

Chapter

12

A PLAN TO PLAN

Many people feel resistance when they hear the word *planning*. It could bring up a feeling of lack of spontaneity, an image of spending countless hours meal planning, or it might seem tedious and frustrating. Maybe you don't think of yourself as a planner, but planning doesn't have to be painful. Think of it as getting excited for, getting ready for, getting the most out of the days of your work and life!

Throughout the first few parts of this book I've shared many tactics. List-making tactics, tactics for refining your calendar, tactics for setting up your days. We've talked about the *what, when,* and *where* of getting things done but the only thing that can make those more effective is planning them out ahead of time. Just as important as any tactic or tool or strategy itself is *how* you execute it. Executing your to-do's is the *Close* portion in the 5 *C's of Productivity,* and arguably the most important! The best way to make sure you're closing all of these loops when you say you will is planning—thinking them through, preparing them for action—*ahead of time.* Planning is so much more than writing things down or just glancing ahead. It's an energy exercise. It's crucial for intention. Last-minute planning—a "day-of" effort—is a recipe for disaster. Planning and preparing before it happens are the keys to success because planning is the direct link to Future You. This is why taking a few minutes to fill out an Hour-by-Hour Plan *the night before* makes a huge difference (like the one below).

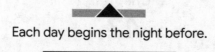

Each day begins the night before.

HOUR-BY-HOUR PLAN

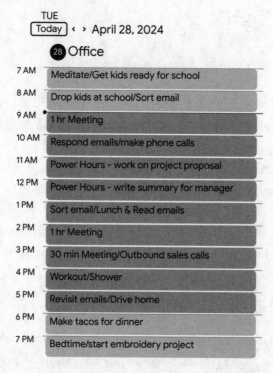

TUE
[Today] ‹ › April 28, 2024

28 Office

7 AM	Meditate/Get kids ready for school
8 AM	Drop kids at school/Sort email
9 AM	1 hr Meeting
10 AM	Respond emails/make phone calls
11 AM	Power Hours - work on project proposal
12 PM	Power Hours - write summary for manager
1 PM	Sort email/Lunch & Read emails
2 PM	1 hr Meeting
3 PM	30 min Meeting/Outbound sales calls
4 PM	Workout/Shower
5 PM	Revisit emails/Drive home
6 PM	Make tacos for dinner
7 PM	Bedtime/start embroidery project

Time to Let It Soak In

Anyone can decide at 4:00 p.m. that they want chicken for dinner. Sure, you can salt it and add some seasoning and toss it on the grill. But what if you had made a plan to grill it last night, so you put it in your favorite marinade overnight, and let it soak all through today until you grilled it up this evening? Planning for the meal ahead of time makes it so much more flavorful and so much more delicious. Just a little intention and one to two additional preparation steps make a huge difference in the end product. Plus while it sits in the sauce all day, you get to anticipate and dream about how delicious it's going to be tonight. Or how fun would a vacation be if I told you, *Hey! You leave tonight—pack your bags!* instead of *Hey! You're going to Fiji a month from today!* In the latter example you get to pick out new swimsuits, look up pictures of Fiji, plan your snorkeling trip, and get excited. While there is value in spontaneous travel, excitement has more time to build when you've made a vacation plan in advance. Things are simply richer when planning is involved—whether it's dinner, a vacation, or your day.

Planning adds value to tasks by letting them *soak in.* In Chapter 3 we talked about the Daily List and how it can be helpful to narrow in on what you need to do. However, so much of the value of the Daily List comes from doing it the night before. It sets you up for the next day by giving you ten to twelve hours to mentally prepare for what you're going to do. If I add an item to my hour-by-hour schedule for the next day at 10:00 a.m., I already know that I'm going to be working on that, at that time. I'm met with much less resistance at 9:59 a.m. when it's time to transition to that activity. I'm already prepared for it. I've already gotten used to the idea that I'll be working on it and may have even brainstormed some ideas I'd like to do for that task already. Planning is another way of lowering the wall of resistance to begin something. It's the no-surprise way for your brain to transition to the next activity, because it was already set out to do it.

Meeting agendas work in a similar marinating way. Let's say you have your regular one-on-one check-in with your manager tomorrow. You'd like to bring up a big-picture career chat. Your manager thinks it's a business-as-usual meeting where you'll give them status updates on your projects. The meeting begins. You spring the career conversation on them. While they could transition to chat about it, their energy was in a *completely* different place so they're having to switch gears. You've missed the window to make it the best conversation possible. That could have been solved with an agenda. Your manager would not only have been prepared for the meeting by coming with the right energy, but they may have even come with thoughts and ideas about your career and things they wanted to say that had come to them ahead of time.

When You See *X*, Plan to *Y*

Another good way to get in the habit of planning is to use the *when I see x, I plan for y* formula. This triggers your brain to say, *Anytime I spot this somewhere, I associate a planning task with it to make sure I'm ready for it.* Some examples I use:

- When I see a meeting invite, I do not delete it from my inbox until I've also blocked any time I need to prepare for it.
- When I see a deadline on a project, I immediately make sure that I've backed into work time to complete it, and included that deadline on my Main List.
- When I get invited to a birthday party or event, I RSVP but leave the invite sitting out until I've purchased a gift.
- When I run out of an item in the kitchen or pantry, I leave the empty packaging on the counter until I've added it to my grocery list so I don't forget to replace it.
- When I receive a gift or a nice letter, I keep the box or envelope sitting out until I remember to write a thank-you note.

Depending on your role or tasks, you can customize these to create planning triggers anywhere you need them.

The More You Plan, the Easier It Gets

Planning gets easier the more you do it. If you plan meals every week, you start to get into a cadence with your favorite recipes—what ingredients you usually use, what you don't have stocked, how long it takes to make each recipe. It's the same with planning for work. Once you plan a few times, you start to learn how long tasks take, when is the best time to slot them, and what gets in the way. You can even start to notice your pitfalls: "I know that Future Me will be mad if I don't plan for extra time to prepare or mentally prep before this meeting, so I'm going to make sure to do that." Or "I know Future Me gets really exhausted after these all-day meetings so I'm going to plan to always have an easy night after that." You start to trust your plan and not have to depend on your memory. It gives your mind more of a chance to relax and come up with new ideas, because it's not holding on to everything you need to do and when. Planning clears the pathways to opening new loops by freeing up that space, and creates that relaxed confidence that you will get the right things done.

Planning isn't an activity to be dreaded or avoided. It's an essential activity that, when done properly, energizes us, enthuses us, and draws us into the future. Not to mention taking the time to plan often saves us time in the long run (like the example from Chapter 3 of shaving time off the grocery store trip by taking time to make a list first). Planning is one of the best gifts that Present You can give to Future You. The future that you plan for—tomorrow or next week or next year—also involves other people, and in the workplace, *other people* means *meetings*.

PRODUCTIVITY PRACTICES

- Create your Daily and Weekly Lists *before* the day or week begins and watch how it shifts your mindset once you're within the day.
- Come up with a few when *I see x, I plan for y* triggers that create a habit of building in time you need or things you need to do *before* they happen.
- Practice planning a few weeks and see how big a difference it makes in your energy, procrastination, and intention.

Chapter

13

MAKE MEETINGS MEETINGFUL

What if I asked you to spend up to twenty-three hours of your time—nearly a full day—doing something next week and told you that it may or may not be a great use of your time? You likely would not commit to doing it—that's a lot of hours to spend on something.

A 2017 *Harvard Business Review* survey found that executives spent an average of *twenty-three hours a week* in meetings, up from less than ten hours in the 1960s. An article in the Massachusetts Institute of Technology's *Sloan Management Review* reported that while the average worker may spend as few as six hours a week in meetings (virtual or in person), supervisors spend more time in meetings than nonsupervisors, and the time that meetings demand increases exponentially as you move up the ladder.

No matter how much time you spend in meetings, they should be an *excellent* use of your time. When meeting quality increases, employees are happier and more satisfied with their jobs (a 2010 study published in *Human Resources Management Journal* found a direct correlation between meeting satisfaction and job satisfaction). Here are some things to think about, whether you're hosting meetings yourself or just attending them.

DO YOU NEED A MEETING?

The first step is to stop and ask, *Is a meeting actually needed?* So many meetings could have been emails or chats. Meetings are an expensive use of time and resources because you're paying a lot of people to be in the same room at the same time.

Think of a ten-person meeting where everyone goes around in a circle and gives a three-minute update about their week. The same thing could have been accomplished by those ten people sending three bullets about their week in a combined email, which would have taken individuals five minutes or less to read on their own time. A meeting is twenty-five minutes more of everyone's time for the same end result!

There's also the opportunity costs. Using the trade-off mindset we looked at in Chapter 2, saying *yes* to a meeting is saying *no* to something else. Any time you spend time in a meeting, you're spending time *not* doing another thing. You always want to make sure that attending a meeting is the best possible use of your time at that moment. Otherwise, it's probably not worth the trade-off.

IS A MEETING UP TO PAR?

If it's decided that a meeting should happen, you want to make sure it's up to PAR:

P: *Purpose*—Why is the meeting happening and what type of meeting is it?

A: *Agenda*—Set and circulate an agenda in advance to help others prepare and determine if they're needed

R: *Result*—Define what a successful conclusion of the meeting looks like and follow up with notes and clear action items

Purpose: Every meeting should have a purpose, and it should be shared with participants ahead of time. In one of my favorite productivity books, *Meetings Suck: Turning One of the Most Loathed Elements of Business into One of the Most Valuable*, author Cameron Herold discusses three types of meetings:

- *Information Sharing*: Upward or downward, not necessarily for discussion or feedback or decisions, just FYI.
- *Creative Discussion*: Or brainstorm. Coming together to elicit a group of ideas, a response to a situation, or a new strategy. No decision will necessarily be made.
- *Consensus Decision*: Something will change after the conclusion of the meeting based on what was decided there.

To those I'd like to add a fourth:

- *Connection*: Especially in the age of virtual, remote, and hybrid work, sometimes a meeting's only purpose is to connect.

Meetings can be (and usually are) a combination of these things, but labeling them when you schedule them helps you and the other attendees decide what is important to think about before and after. A meeting's purpose can span more than one of these categories and should always be clearly communicated to participants.

Agenda: As you know from Chapter 11, I only attend meetings with agendas—and for good reason. There are more benefits to an agenda than just knowing what we'll talk about. Positive effects of an agenda:

- People who think ahead (rather than thinking on the spot) are engaged and have had a chance to process.
- People come with ideas and with the right energy.

- Time is maximized and time waste is avoided. Presenters know how much time they have.
- Attendees can opt out or send delegates based on content so the right people are always in the room.
- Energy is focused in the right place and everyone's in the right frame of mind to talk through the agenda items.
- Attendees come prepared and are on the same page since materials that need reading or review are sent ahead of time.

Meeting name
Attendees (optional)

Purpose(s):
(Select from Information Sharing, Decision Making, Brainstorm or Connection)

Prework or Prep Documents
(Let participants know how long you expect this to take - i.e. 8 min read)

Intended Outcome:
(What would a successful end to the meeting be?)

Agenda:
- Review Action Items from last meeting (if applicable)
- Agenda Item 1 - owner (allocated time - i.e. 10min)
- Agenda Item 2 (allocated time - i.e. 10min)

Result:

Notes:
_____
_____
_____

Follow Up/Action items:
- Action item (Assign an owner)
- Action item (Assign an owner)
- Action item (Assign an owner)

- Agendas are a great place to give a last nudge for outstanding action items and keep people accountable.

The agenda template on the previous page can also be found on my website. With all the positive effects of an agenda, I can't think of a single negative one. I suggest starting with the template that I created for Googlers, which has become widely used.

Result: Arguably the most important part of a meeting is the result: *What would be a successful end to this meeting?* If a meeting is successful the *Intended Outcome* (listed in the template above) will be equal to the *Result*. Many people schedule meetings simply because it feels like the next step. However, if the meeting creator hasn't taken the time to envision what a successful meeting result would be, they shouldn't be asking for the time of others yet. When a meeting does reach a successful result, it should be communicated clearly to participants:

- Decisions or conclusions that are made are clearly restated in the follow-up or wrap-up communication (including *how* and *why* the decision was made, for anyone who wasn't present).
- Next steps and action items are clearly set and communicated, with deadlines.
- Any notes, recordings, or transcripts that need to be shared are sent out for guests who didn't attend or who were optional.

If you're deciding to host a meeting, make sure it's up to PAR before scheduling. If you're part of a meeting that isn't up to PAR, it's okay to ask nicely for an agenda to be sent or a purpose to be defined.

If an individual can attend a meeting and
be on their laptop the entire time, they
probably didn't need to be there.

WHO SHOULD COME?

As the meeting organizer, you should aim for the minimum number of attendees to accomplish the meeting goal. Every person invited should add value, get value, or both. I suggest making the guest list *uncomfortably small* to start because it drives the point that you should start by aiming for the most limited number of guests. Make that your starting point and, after making your original list, continue to evaluate if more guests are needed to get the job done. Different meeting types will call for different group sizes. Aim to include only the people who will be actively engaged; others who would like to know what happened can read the follow-up notes/summary and gather the same information.

If you're not sure who should attend from a team, ask first. You can also add certain individuals as *optional*. Since you'll be sending a clearly defined agenda, anyone on the invite list should be able to discern if they are the right person to attend, or add someone else who is. Using the optional guest feature allows people to opt out and avoids the *I feel like I should invite this person so I will* and the *I feel like I should go because they invited me* conundrum.

Decision-making meetings are particularly important to keep small. In *Decide & Deliver: 5 Steps to Breakthrough Performance in Your Organization*, research by authors Marcia Blenko, Michael C. Mankins, and Paul Rogers confirms the conventional wisdom that once you have seven people in a meeting, each additional person reduces decision effectiveness by 10 percent.

Attending a meeting is not a badge of honor. Make sure your language and actions reflect that. Balance and boundaries are the new busy. If you've included all the important pieces of a meeting agenda and someone declines, *respect it*. They've decided they're not the right person or it's not the best use of their time, and you should feel empowered to do the same.

HOW LONG?

Just as you should start with an uncomfortably small guest list, you should aim for an *uncomfortably short* meeting time, at least initially. Our inclination is to make meetings longer than they need to be, so by starting with the goal to make it short, it will usually end up being the right amount of time. Parkinson's law is the idea that work expands to fill the time allotted for it, and meetings are no different. We've all been in the meeting that was scheduled for an hour, and the set agenda wraps up at around forty-seven minutes; then someone brings up an off-topic item that ends up derailing the conversation, and before you know it the meeting has run ten minutes over! That's what you can avoid by keeping meetings short and to the point.

Because thirty minutes seems to be a standard meeting time, and NBC's *The Office* is a widely known thirty-minute sitcom, I like to use the *Office* Rule when scheduling meetings. I look at the agenda and think, *Do I need an entire episode of* The Office, *including commercials, to talk about what is on this agenda?* If it's a single agenda item, the answer is usually *no*. Thirty minutes is a lot of time to talk about one thing.

Don't be afraid of scheduling fifteen- and forty-five-minute meetings, which can make a big difference in your schedule. Cutting four weekly one-hour meetings to forty-five minutes gives you back an hour of your time. If you have recurring meetings, it's important to consider each of them individually: If one week, there is a lot to talk about, keep the allotted hour. But if the following week there is less on the agenda, don't be afraid to shorten the meeting or ask the host to shorten it. If you are the meeting creator, you can gain respect by canceling and shortening meetings when appropriate. It signals to others that you are acutely aware that you are using their time. Showing up to a meeting you own that's already started and saying, *Well, we didn't have much to discuss today but since we already had this hour on the schedule, I figured we'd check in* is a sure way to make sure that others may not respect or come to your meeting as often in the future.

HOW OFTEN?

The only way to really know how often a meeting should be is to set it for a certain cadence or recurrence, then check in after a while and see if that's the right one. Many people forget the check-in part. They schedule something weekly that goes on for eternity, and then almost never stop to ask themselves if the weekly cadence is correct. Perhaps the meeting goes over often or there are ad hoc meetings happening on the side because the regular check-in is not frequent enough. Conversely, maybe the meeting happens too frequently and so there is not enough on the agenda and more time could pass between instances. Just like the Goldilocks story, you want to test to see if a meeting is too sparse, too frequent, too long, or too short, until it's just right.

One way to take the guesswork out of this is to limit the number of recurrences you have for any meeting series to start. At the beginning, decide you will start by scheduling only five instances of that meeting. At the end of those five instances, you'll be forced to reevaluate (with that Zero-based Calendar mindset) and reschedule the meeting at the same or different cadence and length, or cancel the meeting, as appropriate. If that cadence worked—great! Keep it. If you've noticed that the meeting is stale or really could be shorter—make the change!

After setting the frequency of a meeting, keep the meeting *meetingful*. Let's say you have a weekly check-in with someone, but throughout the week, you instant message or email them any time an idea or non-time-sensitive question comes up, instead of adding it to your check-in agenda. You've now downgraded the reason and quality of that meeting. It's no longer the go-to place for you to connect with that person. Because of your frequent chats and emails throughout the week, you likely won't have much to cover with them at your regularly scheduled check-in. Similarly, if you have a weekly update meeting with your team but also flood their inbox with updates, you've asked both for their time weekly and now for space in their inbox. Honor the cadence you've chosen and, when possible, save communications that can wait until the meeting to increase your meeting's value.

FOLLOW-UP

Follow-up can look different for every type of meeting but should relate to the meeting type. I'm not a huge *exact notes, word-for-word* person because honestly, who reads those? Summarizing key points with bullets, links to important decks, and clear action items with deadlines are most important.

Here are general follow-up guidelines for each of the four types of meeting we discussed:

Information Sharing: Follow-up should include what information was shared and any links or information for additional learning that needs to occur.

Creative Discussion (or Brainstorm): Follow-up should give a summary of what was discussed, a place to send additional ideas if they come to someone after the meeting (this happens often!), and if a decision is to be made with the information discussed, when and how that will be made.

Consensus Decision: Follow-up should include what decision was made and how and when any changes will go into effect. This avoids excessive chatter after a meeting or confusion about when and how a decision was made.

Connection: Follow-up should reaffirm anything discussed, solidify connections if the intent was networking or exploration of opportunities, and possibly set a date for the next connection.

If you receive a follow-up or action item from a meeting, add it directly to your List Funnel. If it's due by the end of the day, find a spot for it in your Daily List. If it's due by the end of the week, put it on your current Weekly List. If it's due more than a week out, add it to your Main List with a deadline and find time for it in the coming weeks!

IS IT AN *EXCELLENT* USE OF TIME?

If you own a meeting (or even if you're a participant) you have the responsibility to make it an *excellent* use of everyone's time. If you're in a meeting that isn't a great use of your time, you have the responsibility to (nicely!) challenge the creator and suggest changes. You can also volunteer your time and effort to make the meeting run smoother, an act that any meeting owner usually appreciates.

The best meeting I've ever attended at Google was a weekly product meeting hosted by a product manager and including all the cross-functional people working on the product. Some of the things that made it so great that I remember it twelve years later:

- The meeting started *exactly* on time with a fun fact or tip or Google perk that was not included in the follow-up notes. People *raced* to get to the meeting on time (even joining from their laptops if they couldn't get in the conference room!) just to hear it.
- Participants were sent an agenda two days before with what was being discussed, pre-reads, and prep. If the agenda items did not add up to the usual hour allotted, the meeting was shortened. If the agenda wasn't enough to warrant a meeting, it was canceled for that week.
- At the beginning of the meeting, it was assumed that every person had read the pre-reads and we did not go over the information or slides that were expected to be read. (If a participant didn't read it the first time, they soon realized they started the meeting behind and did not skip the pre-work ever again!)
- The first item on the agenda every single week was to check in on

the progress of the action items assigned the previous week. I can't tell you how accountable this made people. If you were assigned an action item the week before, you *knew* you were going to be asked about it first thing the following week, so you started working on it immediately. You wanted to have a good update in front of everyone!

- There was an egg timer in the room that went off when presenters had one minute left for their allotted agenda portion. There were no awkward interruptions to cut off presenters—everyone heard the timer and knew what it meant.

I always looked forward to that meeting because I knew it would *never* be a waste of my time. It ran like a well-oiled machine, and the product manager was respected for it. The product thrived because of it. This was a shining example of true meeting excellence.

DON'T GUESS . . . ASK!

Let's say you host a meeting and you're wondering if the meeting is too long or too short, too frequent or infrequent, or if participants feel it's a good use of time. Instead of wondering—it's easier just to ask! Send an anonymous survey or questionnaire for any meeting you own and see what people are saying "behind the meeting's back." Oftentimes it aligns with what you were already thinking. You've been wanting to shorten your staff meeting but you feel like your team won't think they get enough time with you. Meanwhile, they've been hoping for you to shorten it. Make it a habit of getting a feel for any meeting you own and also giving that honest feedback when you're asked as a meeting attendee.

MEETINGS CAN TAKE UP A lot of time, but they can be a good use of time if they're run well. If you're the owner of the meeting, think about things like agenda, follow-up, timeliness, who should be there, how often and how long it should be. If you're attending a meeting, think about these same things and give feedback to the organizer. Everyone respects someone who wants to use their time (and others') wisely. By getting control of your meetings, you get control of your workday.

Setting priorities, learning to say no to things that steal your time, understanding your own energy flow, learning to organize your schedule, and maximizing the quality of your meetings are fundamental building blocks of Uptime. In the preceding chapters we've discussed an abundance of new tactics and tools for making all this happen. The tools you use every day can, with a little customization, be turned into power tools.

PRODUCTIVITY PRACTICES

- Before scheduling a meeting, ask yourself if the meeting is up to PAR, and if it is, what meeting type it falls into.
- Take a hard look at who attends the meeting, how often, and for how long. See if the number of attendees or recurrences, or the length of the meeting, can be reduced.
- Keep meetings "meetingful" by funneling things to the agenda when possible versus initiating another mode of communication.
- Check in on meetings you own and recurring meetings often to see if they are the right cadence and length; send a survey and ask.
- Design an optimal agenda and follow-up model for the meeting.

Chapter

14

TURN YOUR TOOLS INTO POWER TOOLS

In the introduction I talked about productivity often being thought of as *efficiency*—how much you can get done in the least amount of time. While productivity does have a broader definition, being efficient is certainly part of that. Your ability to close loops seamlessly and as quickly as possible does affect how much you get done overall.

Many people rely on tools, like apps and various programs and platforms, to fill in productivity gaps. While tools are great and can certainly enhance overall workflow, it's really the combination of the *intention* behind the tools and *knowing how to use* the tools well that makes them a win for productivity.

In one of my coaching sessions I showed someone who had been using Gmail for work for twelve years how to change the color of the labels on messages. We "popped" emails that he needed to see from his superiors by making them bright red. We added another color to labels for emails coming from outside the company so he could easily prioritize sales emails. He was so excited to have this new visual way to see what was going on in his inbox. Meanwhile, I couldn't help but think how helpful it would have been for him to have learned this earlier and had twelve more years of color-coded emails!

SPEND TIME IN THE SETTINGS

I've sent a weekly email to over fifty thousand Googlers for nine years now with a quick tip about how to be productive in Google Workspace—the communication and collaboration apps used by billions, including Gmail, Google Chat, Calendar, Drive, Docs, Sheets, Meet, and more. My tips, which can now be found on the Google Workspace YouTube channel, cover everything from creating a Google Calendar event directly from Gmail to using images in a Google Form question. They're meant to be small, helpful hints for saving time. I get hundreds of emails from people who have been following these tips for years, telling me how much time it has saved them and how much it has boosted their overall productivity. I also get lots of emails asking, *How do you come up with these?*

Now I am part of the development of many of these features, collaborating with the product teams, and receiving advance notice of their release. However, for the first few years, I found all of my tips in the settings.

The settings of any product or tool are there for just that: to *set* you up for success. To customize, to enhance your workflow, to make the tool *yours*. So many of these features are ignored because we simply fail to spend time with the settings to figure out what they are. For any product you touch once a week or more—from your TV or washing machine to your email or messaging program—you should spend twenty minutes up front digging through the settings to see what it's capable of.

My father-in-law loads his dishwasher with an incredible amount of precision. You wouldn't believe how many dishes he fits in, and they all come out clean. It looks like a carefully curated design each night. He has a certain direction for the bowls and plates to face, the cups lined up in seemingly perfect angles. Not an inch is unused or wasted. I asked him

Spending twenty minutes in your tool's
settings is what turns it into a power tool.

---

how he learned to do it so well, and you can guess what he said. He read
the manufacturer's instructions on how to pack the dishwasher. Who
does that? Almost no one. But what if we all did? Every single night
would be made easier by fitting more dishes and having them all come
out clean. What a small upfront investment for such a big daily payoff.

What if we did this for all of our tools at work—like our email, our
messaging program, and our calendar? We could know everything about
how to customize our notifications on our mobile devices to see only
what we want, when we want it, and how to color-code, tag, and find
what we need. Most of us dive into using these tools without fully exploring what they can do and become entrenched in using them every
day without learning how powerful they can truly be.

CUSTOMIZE WHAT YOU SEE, OR DON'T SEE

We'll talk more about this in the next chapter, but one big part of making
your products work for you is making sure they don't work *against* you.
Sometimes your productivity tools and programs can inadvertently decrease your productivity by distracting you with notifications. The opportunities are endless for how and when you can be notified that something
needs your attention. Anything that gets your attention for a second or
more chips away at your overall brain space, even if you don't open the
notification or follow through on it—it still takes a few of those energy
points. That adds up.

Make sure you're taking advantage of any customization that allows
you to control what you see, especially with devices that are with you all
the time. On your phone you can control what calls you see, when your

phone rings, what hours it rings, and the volume and tone of the ring, and the same goes for email or message notifications. Consider setting up a notification digest or customize notifications to see instant messages only during your work hours. Figure out how to be notified if *certain* people email you, but not for everyone. You could set up a time to get the top news headlines once a day, instead of receiving an update every time there is a new alert throughout the day. I limit the social media apps on my phone to just one hour at night (I even asked my husband to control the passcode to change it so I'm not tempted to!). All of these small changes within the settings of a product help create a cleaner mental space for creativity and opening loops and avoiding the constant chatter.

MAKE IT PERSONAL

In addition to customizing settings, customize design! You are way more likely to keep something organized and managed if it appeals to you. It's more motivating to make your bed when you love the comforter! It's more pleasing to look at your email when you've changed the background to your favorite beach picture. Color-coding your folders in a file management system makes it more visually interesting. I once worked with an executive who was most excited that I taught him how to add a plane emoji next to all of the flights on his virtual calendar, and a tennis ball on the events for his daughter's tennis matches. When you're looking at things like your tools, your programs, your email, your desk, and your calendar multiple times every day, finding small things that visually please you makes a difference.

Tom Oliveri, VP of the CEO team at Google, has a huge number of things come across his desk every day. There are emails, lists, presentations to review, and decisions to be made. He also happens to have a love of burritos. His assistant, Sarah, wanted a way to get his attention to flag things that were most important. So when there was a lot going on, she sent him an email with one single subject line: a burrito emoji 🌯. Since Tom is such a fan of burritos for lunch, he found it amusing. It became something fun that was noticeable and representative but still helped get the point across, "this is important," within his team. Soon this email was referred to as "The Burrito List," which feels much more fun to interact with than "The To-Do List." For Tom this little bit of fun and customization of his tool made a small difference in his day and workflow. Taking the time to find and customize your workflows this way breaks up the mundane and helps you stick with a tool or system.

HARNESSING THE POWER OF AI TO WORK SMARTER

It's no secret that artificial intelligence (AI) is already transforming the world of work and how we get things done. Generative AI, which can generate new outputs from simple prompts, can already help people write or revise emails and documents, summarize information, and even create images, videos, and presentations from scratch. My approach to using gen AI in a solution like Google Workspace is the same as it is for understanding your settings—get to know upfront what the tools can do for you. But AI isn't foolproof and it works best when it's combined with human feedback. So maybe you experiment with letting your favorite gen-AI tool take a pass at developing the project summary or the presentation slides, and then provide feedback to make it better. Read the settings of your tools to find out how AI is integrated and what prompts you can use with it. Once you have a starting point you can typically adjust tone, voice, and length very easily, and then add your own manual touches. At the end of the day, AI is no replacement for the ingenuity, creativity, and smarts of real people. But there's no doubt it has become one of our best power tools—if used thoughtfully—and will continue to improve productivity in the years ahead.

TAKE THE SHORTCUT

Perhaps the most obvious element of interacting effectively with your devices is knowing the shortcuts for how to move around faster. Keyboard shortcuts, which allow you to perform common actions without touching your mouse, are the unsung heroes of the productivity world. For example, in Gmail, once shortcuts are enabled in the settings, simply pressing r replies to an email, a replies to all—these are just a few of many. Every program has keyboard shortcuts and they can shave seconds if not minutes off common actions. A calculation by the education platform Brainscape estimated that by learning keyboard shortcuts for your top daily actions, you could save up to sixty-four hours—*eight working days*—each year. Many people who sit behind me or in my cube watch me work and ask, *How did you do that so fast? How did you flip from one tab to another without touching your mouse?* My answer is always *Keyboard shortcuts!*

Start with something small, like your email. Think of the top actions that you do in a day (reply, reply all, delete, archive). Figure out and practice the keyboard shortcuts for those top actions. Even something like learning the keyboard shortcut to open a new window in your browser could shave minutes off your day depending on how often you do it.

If you really want to be hard-core, put yourself in keyboard shortcut boot camp. This means actually disabling your mouse, or turning it upside down, or putting it away. Every time you go to touch your mouse, use the keyboard shortcut to bring up the keyboard shortcut menu, and figure out how to do it with a key. I had a spreadsheets class at UNC Chapel Hill where they came around to disable our mouses for the final exam and everything had to be done with shortcuts. Memorizing those shortcuts once has made them stick with me for years. As someone who uses spreadsheets daily, think of all the time they have saved me over the course of more than a decade. All because I put in a small amount of time for that exam to really learn all of them up front.

As relatively minor as these tips and hints might seem, I wouldn't have devoted a chapter to them if I didn't know from experience—my own and that of the thousands of people I've worked with—what an enormous amount of time they can save you, and how that time savings can allow you to move forward at a pace and level of productivity that were previously unimaginable. No matter how swiftly you move, distractions can still attempt to get in your way. In the next chapter we'll discuss how to get ahead of distractions before they come, and how to handle them if they do.

PRODUCTIVITY PRACTICES

- Think of a few things you use every day, like your phone, your email program, and your dishwasher. Spend twenty minutes in the settings poking around to figure out what it can do for you.
- Customize your notifications and tools to show you only the things you want to see, when you want to see them. Customize them further to make them something that you find visually pleasing!
- Find your top three to five actions in your top-used products and learn the keyboard shortcuts to shave time off your regular activities.

Chapter

15

GET AHEAD OF DISTRACTIONS

If you've identified your priorities, made the time to work on them, made sure it's at your best time of day in the right location, and made sure you know your tools well . . . things will get done, right? Not always. Enter *distractions*. As I mentioned in the introduction, Flow + Focus = Time Better Spent. When you've made a perfect bubble to get things done, the time and energy may be there, but unless focus is there, too, you can't guarantee Uptime.

Being *heads down, in the flow,* or doing *deep work*—all of these popular phrases allude to the same state: work without distraction. These days, it can be hard to find focus. We're mentally—and often physically—working in multiple locations. We're learning how to communicate and collaborate in all those spaces. And we're inundated with a constant flow of notifications, alerts, and interruptions, often from the very technology that's supposed to help us be productive! A study by the University of California, Irvine found that it takes an average of twenty-three minutes and fifteen seconds to regain focus after a distraction. It's no wonder we find it difficult to achieve that work zone.

It's hard to sweep a distraction to the side once it comes up. You can't count on yourself not to engage with pings, chats, texts, or emails once you see them—and that's okay! The easier method is to do everything you can to *prevent* distractions from entering your workspace at all.

**The best way to deal with a
distraction is before it happens.**

CHILDPROOFING YOUR WORKSPACE

Similar to Chapter 7, where we discussed acting as your own assistant, when it comes to distractions, take that removed, third-party view of your own workflow. I think of this *setting the scene* for working without distraction as similar to the act of childproofing your home.

Imagine you have a small child coming over to your house for a week. This child is old enough to walk around and get into everything but young enough to not understand instructions. You have three options:

1. Do nothing to prepare for the child's visit. Chase the child around for the entire week and watch them closely for every safety hazard. *Don't grab that knife out of the drawer! Don't touch the open fireplace! Don't put your finger in that plug!* And so on . . .
2. Designate one safe room or area and strictly allow the child only in that room.
3. Childproof! Take a few minutes to close the fireplace grate, plug up the plugs, lock the knife drawer, and remove any hazards off the floor, giving the child freedom to explore.

You can see that while option 3 takes a little more effort up front, it makes for a more relaxing week. Option 2 is a good quick fix, but can be limiting and unrealistic especially for a longer period of time. Option 1 sounds exhausting. By the third day you would be utterly depleted. Your brain is on all the time, scanning, watching, trying to catch things in the moment and redirect—talk about losing energy points! Not to mention it's much more likely that something unsafe would happen.

The same goes for how you approach focus at work. The coordinating options look like:

1. Do nothing to prepare for a focused-work block. Allow access to all notifications, emails, pop-ups, messages, and open tabs. Work with your phone next to you. Hope that if something diverts your attention you have the ability to quickly redirect (which is unlikely, based on research).

2. Establish an environment in which you can see only what you're doing. Print the slides or contract that you need to review and do it on paper. Use a separate computer that doesn't have Wi-Fi or isn't signed in to your usual programs (okay for a short time but unrealistic long term).

3. Act like your own assistant. Take some time to set yourself up for success *before* your work time begins. Think of all the things that could distract Future You in the work block. Use the restroom. Get a snack. Refill your water bottle. Close or minimize all windows and tabs except exactly what you need to work on (I call this *one-tab working*). Turn off pop-up notifications and sign out of messaging programs. Set your phone in another room, more than twenty seconds away. (In his book *The Happiness Advantage: How a Positive Brain Fuels Success in Work and Life*, Shawn Achor introduces the twenty-second rule for habit breaking: If something takes less than twenty seconds to do, you're more likely to do it, and less likely if it takes more than twenty seconds. So make sure the things you don't want interrupting you are more than twenty seconds away.)

As you can see, option 3 is what sets you up for the *most* success for the longest period of time. At first, you may feel almost panicky because your brain is likely conditioned to prefer "video game mode" on high alert looking for stimuli flying toward you that can be swatted away (chats, pop-up notifications, emails). But of course, that uses more energy points from your work blocks. Sitting with a blank document and a pulsing cursor where you're supposed to be writing something can feel much more "boring" at first, but you want to *bore yourself into focus*. Once your brain moves past that original panic (because there is nothing to do other than what you need to do) and is void of distractions, you quickly drop into Uptime mode and get things done in less time.

DON'T LET EMAIL "SUCK" YOU IN

In the next chapter we'll go deep into detail on how to organize and manage your email. But in the context of distractions, it's important to remember that you will likely never, ever, ever, ever open your email and think, *Oh great, nothing to do here at all!* For many of us, emails never stop coming in, and in a way that's a good thing, because it means there's always more to do and accomplish in our jobs or in our lives. The problem happens when we turn on the *email vacuum* too many times a day and let it suck us in. We leave the vacuum on, even on a tab in the background, or constantly pulled up on our phones, and we're always distracted by that noise. Many times we are checking our email when we don't actually plan to do anything about it; we're just looking to see what's there. Remind yourself that every time you look at email, you are inviting it into your brain, using energy points, and giving yourself the opportunity to be distracted.

In my coaching, I find that asking people to check email only two or three times a day is unrealistic. For many, their jobs require that they see email more often than that, because they need to be able to respond promptly. Instead, one habit that can really stick is closing your email once or twice a day to accomplish non-email work. That one small habit (which you can also see outlined in the Daily List worksheet) can make a huge difference in your daily productivity. Ideally this time to close email would be during your Power Hours, when you have the best chance to get things done well, without the noise.

MONOTASKING IS THE NEW MULTITASKING

The promise of multitasking used to be popular in the productivity world but has since proven ineffective. Many productivity tools were designed to help us do many things at once but have since shifted to finding ways to tune out and focus on one thing at a time. Instead of taking my word for it, try this activity.

1. Grab a piece of paper, a pen or pencil, and a timer.
2. Time yourself writing the following:

MULTITASKING

1 2 3 4 5 6 7 8 9 10

3. Flip the paper over to a blank side (so you can't copy your original text or the text in this book).
4. Time yourself writing the same thing, but alternating between the letter and number lines (so M, then 1, then U, then 2) until you make it through both lines.
5. Note the difference in your times.

When I do this in a large group I ask people to raise their hand when they are finished and I stop my timer when the last hand is raised. On average it takes *more than double* the time for the group to complete step 4 than it does step 2, but when you look at both sides of the paper, the output is *exactly the same*. From this unscientific test we can infer that it can take more than twice the amount of time when you're switching between activities. The additional time is needed because it takes longer for our brain to reorient itself and we're using energy points with each switch (letters, now numbers, now letters, now numbers). We're doing

▰▰▲▰▰

**Doing multiple things at once is
doing multiple things poorly.**

---

the same thing to ourselves when we're doing two things at once. *Okay document I'm writing, okay email, okay document, okay instant message, okay document, okay text on my phone.* We are actually taking *more than double the time* to create the same output, likely doing it worse, and wasting energy along the way.

There is a time and place for multitasking: when you're doing one or more mindless activities where the stakes are low regarding the quality of the output. You can wash dishes *and* listen to a podcast. You can take a phone call on your walk. You *could* dial into a meeting that doesn't require your participation while you check emails—but see Chapter 13 for why you probably should have declined that meeting in the first place and read the notes after! While training yourself to focus is the most effective first step, later on we'll dive more into tools like meditation that make focus even easier and more natural. Keep in mind, anytime you care about a task, care about doing it well, and want to do it in the least amount of time: *Do one task only.*

We've seen that preparation (in the form of clearing time and space for Future You by acting as your own assistant) and monotasking are the principal keys to working without distraction. Ironically the chief sources of distraction in today's workplace are also the very things that help us complete our jobs so effectively—the computer and the smartphone. Both of these tools didn't even exist a generation or two ago and we've had to learn new rules to navigate them. The pings, texts, chats, and messages moving across myriad platforms form an endless tsunami of information that we value, and distraction that we don't. One significant stream within that tsunami is email, which deserves its own chapter.

PRODUCTIVITY PRACTICES

- Act as your own assistant and set the scene for distractionless work. Scan for possible distractions and handle them before they happen. Bore yourself into focus.
- Close your email/message program a few times a day to experience the feeling of disconnectedness and focus, especially during Power Hours.
- Show yourself that multitasking loses time. Time yourself doing the MULTITASKING exercise and prove it with the data.
- When you care about the results of a task, do one task only.

Chapter

16

MASTERING EMAIL: THE LAUNDRY METHOD

When I first begin working with a client, we almost always start with email. This is because email, for so many people, is personal. It can be the starting place for work anxiety and is sometimes the single greatest pain point. For many, it's the first thing they see when they wake up, and the last thing they see before they go to bed (including their partner, who is in the bed next to them!). Email is the thing that wakes people up at night thinking, *Did I forget to respond to this?* When it's in your inbox, it's in your head.

For many of us, email started as a convenient asynchronous communication method but has become the thing we spend the most time on, the most time in, and the most time stressing about. It has become a way for other people to add to our to-do lists. As we increasingly move to remote work environments, the number of emails has skyrocketed. Data from the software company HubSpot says email volume has increased by 44 percent since the shift to remote work started by the pandemic.

Email is an effective and necessary communication method. If I'm in my Power Hours, head down and focused on something, and you are in a different time zone fast asleep, we can still effectively create output on a project together by emailing about it. Email provides a record in case others need to be added to the project or if work needs to be shared. While simultaneously editing documents and instant chats can be used for some of these needs, email still holds an important and necessary place in a typical workflow.

Studies have shown that people check email at work around eleven times per hour. Many of those times we're not actually doing anything about it—just checking! In Chapter 3, I encourage closing email once or twice as part of the Daily List, and in Chapter 14, I emphasize the importance of customizing notifications to decrease interruptions. Most importantly, when we do decide to check email, we want to make sure we're making the *most* of that time. Sometimes we are swimming around opening random unread emails, half-completing tasks, fishing for new messages, half-drafting responses, and feeling like we're never really finished. Instead, you want to *do email well.*

You can change your relationship with email using a three-step process I have developed. My email training has been taken by tens of thousands of Googlers and is consistently one of the highest-rated trainings at the company. When I offer this training, I get emails all the time that say things such as: "Wow, you've shaved 30 percent off my time in my inbox!" "I feel so much better" or "I feel totally on top of my email now." "My team has noticed that, after taking this, I'm so much more responsive and on top of my work." Or "I'm sleeping better because I know exactly what's in my email and I know I'm not missing anything!"

THREE STEPS TO CLEAN UP YOUR INBOX

These three steps should be done in order to clean up your inbox. If you did only step 1, that would be enough to feel a difference. If you move to step 2, even better. If you complete step 3, you're golden. You will feel *completely* in control of your email (and that is a good feeling!).

1. **Remove what you don't need to see.** Many times people announce their email count like a badge of honor. *I have 890 unread emails* or *I have thousands of emails in my inbox!* What this usually tells me is either 1) you're missing 890 emails that were sent directly to you, which must mean a lot of frustrated coworkers, or 2) you're getting a lot of emails that you don't actually need to land in your inbox. Usually it's the latter. *Emails in your inbox that you don't open are like clothes you don't wear in your closet.* It's not impressive to have 890 shirts that you don't wear anymore because they don't fit or are out of style. If anything, this makes deciding what to wear *way* more stressful. Your attention is drawn to these clothes even if they never leave the hanger. You're using way more energy points to mentally sort through and find a shirt to wear than if those unused clothes weren't there. Similarly in email, every message in your inbox uses some of your energy points, even if you do not open it. Once it's in your inbox, that **bold** font tricks your brain into thinking there is something you have to do with it, whether you ever open it or not.

Every email that hits your inbox takes
a tiny piece of your attention and
energy, even if you never open it.

Your goal for step 1 is to get as many of those unneeded emails as possible out of your inbox. Create filters or rules in your email program to have them **never hit the inbox**. See how your attention was drawn to that phrase because it was bolded? Same goes for those subject lines of things you don't need to care about that hit your inbox **unread**. For many people, those unread emails come in the form of newsletters or alerts they've inadvertently signed up for. A quick way to capture all those is to search your inbox for words like *unsubscribe* or *view in browser*. Those keywords are typically in emails that came from mailing lists and weren't sent directly to you. You can use those search items to make rules or filters that those emails never hit your inbox, or once you've found those emails, follow through on their instructions to unsubscribe.

Set a timer for thirty minutes, and treat it like a game where the goal is to see how many emails you can eliminate. Find every email that shouldn't ever have been seen by you and find a way to keep it from happening again: create a filter, block the sender, unsubscribe from the mailing list, or mark it as spam. This purging is similar to getting rid of all those clothes you don't wear anymore. Checking your inbox will feel like pure *ahhh* after you take the time to see only what you need to see.

2. **Make what you *do* need to see stand out.** If the CEO of your company emails you directly, that email should appear differently than the emails that the CEO broadcasts to the whole company. An email from your professor sent directly to you should look different than one she sends to the whole class. An email from your child's principal to you should look different than the weekly school newsletter they send. If you have a lot of meetings or travel often, and as a result look at emails mostly or primarily on your mobile phone (whose inbox is smaller and less detailed than what you see on your computer screen), you should know what things need to be opened immediately as opposed to things that can wait until later. You can tell Future You a lot about what is inside an email before it's ever opened and use fewer energy points constantly scanning your inbox to find what's important. Create labels or flags like *VIP* or *Urgent Notification* and then have them applied automatically using filters or rules. In Gmail this looks like adding a label automatically to an email using a filter rule. For example, if it's from my manager, sent directly to me, *give it this label*. If it's from my largest sales client (*@clientdomain.com) then mark it as a bright and bold

label (still have it come right to my inbox, just a different color than the rest). Let your email program do the work of prioritizing by automatically flagging things, so that with a quick scan you have a visual landscape of what is in your inbox before opening anything. Creating a few of these rules sets Future You up to never miss an important email, and to have visual cues that help you partially prioritize things before even reading the subject lines.

3. **Sort your email like you sort your laundry.** Forget email for a second, let's talk about something most people understand more— laundry. What if I asked you to go to your dryer to do your laundry like this:

- You open the dryer door and pick out one shirt.
- You fold that shirt and walk all the way upstairs and put it in your dresser, then walk back downstairs to the dryer.
- You find another shirt, fold it, walk upstairs to the dresser, then walk back downstairs to the dryer.
- You find a pair of pants, and it still seems a little damp, but you throw it back in with the other dry clothes.
- You find one sock and don't really feel like hunting for the other sock, so you walk it upstairs and put it in your sock drawer, and come back downstairs.
- You find a pair of pants—oh wait, it's the same pair of damp pants you already touched and you put them back in again.
- You decide you don't really feel like emptying the dryer completely, so you just turn back on the cycle and start over when new clothes are added from the washer.
- You panic every time you need a specific piece of clothing because you don't know if it's in the dryer with all those other clothes, or if you forgot to wash it, or if you actually put it away.

- All throughout the day you leave your dryer door open so you can see all the clothes and remind yourself that you're not done doing laundry.

How inefficient is this? Talk about a waste of energy points! It's a terrible, stressful way to do laundry. Yet this is how many people do email. Wet clothes are thrown back in with the dry clothes (*mark as unread*). The dryer is never emptied (*inbox zero*). People look at their full dryer multiple times throughout the day reminding themselves there's a big mess in there that is not taken care of (*checking email fifteen or more times a day without clearing it*). They wake up in the middle of the night having no idea if they answered an email or if they missed something important in their inbox (*where is that pink shirt??*). So what can the laundry metaphor teach us about managing our email?

- We decide we are *doing email* just as we decide we're *doing laundry*, and set aside specific time for it instead of poking around constantly.
- We address everything in the inbox at one time until we're done, like emptying the dryer.
- We sort it into piles. Similar to *Fold/Hang/Socks That Need Matching*, think *Respond/Read/Revisit*.
- We do all of a pile at one time: *Fold all clothes/Read all articles*, and get the benefits of batch tasking.
- We touch clothes/emails two times *maximum* (the first time we sort it and the next time we reply/fold it), minimizing the energy points we spend on each email.
- We treat sorting/reading/answering as distinct activities, and do not intermix them (instead of folding one shirt, then hanging one dress, then matching socks).
- Even if we don't have time to hang all the clothes (respond

to all the emails), we have a pile of clothes to hang and if
we're missing the green shirt (that one email from our boss),
we know exactly where it is and that it's been touched
once.

SO HOW DOES THIS LOOK IN YOUR INBOX?

Set up your inbox so that you have a separate dryer (main inbox where
everything comes in) and laundry baskets (labels or folders that are not
in the inbox) for different tasks. *You should never have new, unread emails
in the same place that you have emails you've read, but still need action from
you.* Mixing these is like leaving all the dry pants you need to fold in
the dryer with wet socks. How confusing! It's also too confusing to have
multiple dryers. Some people like to have an inbox for internal emails,
another for external emails, and still others for different incoming emails.
However, a tried-and-true productivity principle is *the more places you
have to check, the more stressful the process.* If you had nine mailboxes
outside your house—one for bills, one for advertisements, one for personal cards, and six more for other categories—it would be such a chore
to walk to each mailbox every day. Emptying a single mailbox each day
and sorting what's there is much easier, which is why I don't recommend
having different inboxes for incoming emails.

In Gmail you can create labels for your "baskets" and use Multiple
Inboxes to display those labels so you can see them all at the same time
as your "dryer" (main inbox). In other email programs you can create
folders. The four essential laundry baskets or labels to create are based
on the actions that can be taken with an email:

1. **Respond:** This is something that requires a response from you, and
    needs you and your time to complete.
    Example: Your boss asks for a status update on an important project.
2. **Read:** Something that you'd like to read, but don't need to respond to.
    Example: Industry newsletters, FYI emails, interesting case studies.

3. **Revisit:** This is something that you cannot immediately respond to because you're waiting for a specific time to check in or you're waiting for someone else to respond. Think of these as things you're waiting for or need to follow up on but they're not *your* to-do list.

   Example: You owe an answer to your client but first you need to get Filipe to approve their contract. Your email with Filipe is one you need to revisit if he doesn't respond to you.

4. **Relax:** This means you're done with it! This is where all emails are put to rest. It means things are complete with that action item and now it is archived (can be searched for later), put in some sort of reference folder, or deleted.

   Example: Someone on your team reports successful completion of a task or project.

Respond	Read	Revisit	Relax!
To: You From: Your Manager Subject: The Preso Hi, Great preso today!!! Can you make the changes we talked about and send back ASAP? Thanks! Lanaeschia	To: You From: Morning News Subject: Top Headlines Update on company Cool Tip	To: You From: Filipe Subject: Permit approval Hey you, I'm hoping to have those mobile permits you requested approved by next week. Stay tuned!!! Filipe	To: You From: Your teammate Subject: Great job! So glad we are done with that project. It was great working with you—thanks again!

YOUR DAILY EMAIL WORKFLOW

To switch to this system you'll do a one-time setup where you will put any active emails in your inbox in *Respond, Read,* or *Revisit* and then do a big archive or delete of the rest. *If it doesn't need one of these actions, it doesn't need to stay in your inbox* (more on filing emails away later on). More important than doing a one-time switch to this structure is understanding how to use it every day. You want to think of sorting, *Responding,*

Reading, and *Revisiting* as separate activities, just as sorting your laundry, folding clothes, hanging clothes, and matching socks are different activities. Do not mix them.

Every day pick a time (I find morning works best) to go through your inbox and quickly sort new emails into these four baskets. In Gmail, you can use tools like Auto Advance—going to the next email automatically—and keyboard shortcuts to power through quickly. You should think of this part of your day as *just* sorting emails, and answering only emails that take less than three minutes. On your Hour-by-Hour Plan you should have blocked time for this. The action of emptying your inbox into baskets is what I refer to as *inbox zero* (or *dryer empty*). Everything is pulled out and put into piles. You've now set up Future You by establishing *exactly* what needs to be done with that email. Opening an email and marking it as unread, just like throwing that wet pair of pants back in with the dry clothes, actually frustrates Future You because you're going to have to open and decide on that email yet again—a waste of energy points. *Wait, did I open this? Did I answer it? What was I supposed to do with it again?* This is how people end up touching an email five or six times before it's completed.

Once you've gotten to *inbox zero*, you should find/schedule the time throughout the day (also included in your Hour-by-Hour Plan) to isolate your baskets and look *only* at what you need to do in that basket. Look *only* at your *Respond* emails—block everything else out—and respond! Then during the time you've scheduled to read emails—look *only* at your *Read* basket and do those. When you look at your main inbox it should only contain new emails that have come in since you last sorted; you can re-sort those two to four additional times a day to maintain that *inbox zero*.

Putting things in baskets is a great way of *batch tasking*. You find efficiency and use fewer overall energy points as you perform similar actions all at once. By the fifth shirt you've folded in a row, you're better at folding shirts because you're in the groove. The same goes for responding to five emails in a row, or reading five emails. Doing them together, rather than sporadically throughout the day, gets you in the "mood" of it and creates efficiency.

You should also think of matching these email baskets to your energy levels. If I have an uninterrupted hour during my Power Hours and really want to craft some thoughtful responses, that's a great time to isolate just my *Respond* laundry basket and answer those. If I have two meetings with just a fifteen-minute break in between, I probably won't be able to answer any of my *Respond* emails, but it's a great time to dive into my *Read* basket and scan through some industry news. The end of the day or the end of the week is a great time to quickly go through the *Revisit* basket before I close my laptop for the day.

Once you've addressed any one of these things and it no longer needs to be in that action basket, take it out! Put it wherever you archive or delete or folder away emails. That way your inbox and emails tagged with the next action are the only things you need to see and are the only *active* emails you have. (See figure below for an example of an Hour-by-Hour Plan with email blocks, using these four sorting baskets.)

8:30 am	Get coffee, sit down, sort your inbox to zero using keyboard shortcuts
9:00	Open Respond folder and reply to those emails uninterrupted
10:30	Meeting
11:00	Meeting
11:45	Sort inbox to zero again using keyboard shortcuts
12:00 pm	Lunch
1:00	Finish Respond and work on non-email tasks
1:30	Meeting
2:00	Open Read folder to look at articles
2:30	Meeting
4:00	Open Revisit folder and follow up on anything that needs a reply, sort back to inbox zero before heading home

This system helps you master and maintain your email deluge on an ongoing basis and, most importantly, it's a system you can trust. You create mental clarity by knowing *exactly* where that pink shirt is when you need to find it (or that email from your boss that you need to respond to by next week). Having the laundry baskets full of things that you've touched but haven't finished yet is just as empowering as knowing the things you've already responded to because you know just where you stand with your email. You know whether you need to carve out additional time to go through your baskets if they start getting full. This system puts you in full control and changes your relationship with your inbox. It's an important part of your path to Uptime.

WHERE DO ACTIONS LIVE?

With the Laundry Method for managing your inbox and the List Funnel for all of your to-do's, many people wonder how they play together. If there is something for you to *do* in an email you receive—where does that open loop go—in your *Respond* folder or on your Main List? This will depend a lot on your role or workflow but most people have two action lists going at once and work off both: their Main List and their *Respond* folder. My golden rule is to ask the question, *To resolve this action, where is my work going to be done?* If the work I need to do for the action is responding to the email, I leave it in my *Respond* folder and that's my reminder to respond. However, if the email says, *Please build this new presentation and share with your colleagues,* now this is an action *outside* of my email so I'm going to add it to my Main List (or Weekly List if it's due this week, Daily List if it's due today, etc.). Some people have such a small amount of actions in their email that it actually makes sense to add them all to their Main List. Others may have a job that's *mostly* responding to emails and therefore they're only going to work out of their email folders and need no other list. Maybe chats are the primary method of communication for your team and in that case you manage your chats and pull action items out of your messaging program onto your Main List. Whatever way works best for you, if you're using email you want to make sure that you're adding a slot in your schedule to address each basket as part of your Hour-by-Hour Plan each day (*Read, Review,* and *Respond* labels). Don't fall into the common trap of having email be the thing you never intentionally make time for and expect to squeeze in around everything else. Instead, schedule a "meeting" with your inbox at least once each day.

SEARCH IS THE NEW FOLDERS

Another way to save time in your email is to stop filing away every completed email into folders or labels. Many clients I work with come to me with a process of filing away all or many of their completed emails into folders. This was a common practice at the beginning of emails because we were used to filing papers this way in a physical file folder system. However, you *can't* easily sort through 4,500 pieces of paper to find a paper with certain words, so a filing system was necessary. You *can* easily search 4,500 emails, so the idea that everything should be sorted away into folders is outdated. You're actually using more energy points to sort something into a folder, then finding it, than you would be just searching for it when you need it. One study by IBM suggests that you actually save 54 percent of your time searching for email in a large group versus filing everything up front to find it in those folders later.

Instead of filing completed emails into folders, archive any emails you might need later into *one* large holding place; in Gmail it's called *All Mail.* Then learn the search functions for your email program really well. For example, in Gmail you can search specifically for an email that is between two dates, from a certain person, has or doesn't have certain phrases, and even down to the file size of the attachment. Filing emails into folders does have its place but it's limited. Instead of "every email from my boss" or "every email from my child's school," think instead "new sales pitch ideas" or "recipes I want to try." Maybe if you're a manager, you have a folder for each person on your team and put emails in there that will help you write their performance review. Any labels/folder you make for filing should be for *a group of emails that are difficult to search for* and that you will reference *at a point in time*, like when it's time to write that annual review or when it's time to try a new recipe!

GET TO THE POINT AND RESPOND

When it comes to writing and responding to emails, I like to *send* the type of email that I would want to *receive*. I love when emails are short, friendly, to the point, bulleted, have the ask clearly stated up front (and maybe even summarized again at the bottom), and include a deadline if applicable. If you feel annoyed when you receive an email that links out to a list that could have been included in the body of the email, remember that feeling and, when writing your own email, include your list in the email instead of linking out! Email writing is a great chance to use tools like Duet AI to get a starting point for what you'd like to say. Ask for what you want then iterate.

Respond to all emails within twenty-four hours, but don't *complete* all emails within twenty-four hours.

Nobody enjoys working with someone who is unresponsive to their emails. And a lot of inefficiencies in email come from people "checking back in" or bumping up an email because they haven't heard back from someone. If you don't respond to an email, it usually ensures you'll get another email (more energy points!). As we talked about in Chapter 11, that pressure continues to build. Another email is then followed by an instant chat to get your attention, which turns into a meeting added to your calendar. Instead, avoid this trickle by *responding* to emails promptly. *Responding* does not mean completing the action requested of you! It means acknowledging that you received the email and what you plan to do about it or when you plan to get back to them fully. Responses could be:

> *Hey! I got your request and need to think about it this week—I'll let you know next week.*

> *Thanks for your email—I have time scheduled next Tuesday to work on this so I'll get back to you Wednesday next week.*

> *Hi! This is on my radar but I'm not sure when I'll get to it, if you don't hear from me in the next month or so feel free to follow back up.*

Just responding immediately in this way and then adding it to your *Respond* folder can prevent the guessing game of *Did this person see my email? Did they forget? Should I reach out again on another platform?*

Also use the best practice of checking *back* in as you're working on things and save yourself the check-in email from them.

> *Hey! Still waiting on approval before I can get to this—stay tuned!*

> *Hi! Haven't forgotten about this! Work-in-progress!*

Everyone just wants to know that you received their email, that you're working on it, and when they can expect an answer or deliverable. They just want to be *heard*. People who preemptively check in and respond to email in this way set themselves apart as being "on top of it." Everyone likes to work with a person who has this email practice, personally or professionally! The way you respond to emails (or don't) can be a huge part of people's perception of you in or outside your workplace. No one likes collaborating with a person who doesn't respond to emails. Create a *"reputation of responsiveness"* by being on top of your email, even if you're not *completing* all of them right away.

Mastering email, meetings, time, distraction, and the other things we've discussed in the preceding chapters are all important elements of the new productivity. As we incorporate these tools and techniques into our work, we not only find that we are more productive and less stressed, but we can also see benefits that extend beyond the workplace. That's what we'll explore in the final section of the book.

PRODUCTIVITY PRACTICES

- Get email that you don't need to see out of your inbox with filters and rules.
- Highlight emails you *do* need to see from VIPs, important clients, or important listservs.
- Create three laundry baskets for your email (*Respond/Read/Revisit*) and get things out of the dryer (main inbox) into those baskets, achieving *inbox zero*. Go through the laundry baskets daily and take appropriate action on the emails, making sure you have scheduled time for this on your calendar.
- Learn your email program's search functions instead of filing emails away in folders.
- Write emails that are clear and to the point, using AI as a starting point.
- Reply to emails quickly just to let the sender know that you received the email, what you plan to do about it, and when.

PART V

How to Live Well While Doing It All

Chapter

17

WHEN:THEN ROUTINES

If there's one thing I've learned from leading productivity workshops, coaching executives, and being a parent, it's that *people love routines*. Whether it's an annual holiday tradition, a monthly movie night, a weekly favorite meal, or simply a bedtime ritual, routines create rhythm in our lives, and this rhythm is something we can capitalize upon.

A 2006 Duke University study found that approximately 45 percent of our daily behaviors are habits. While there's a huge trend these days on forming or stopping *habits* (things you do without thought), I like to focus on creating *routines* (natural next-step actions) instead. Habits require motivation, whereas routines flow naturally with intention.

As I mentioned in Chapter 3, starting your week by saying *I have to cook dinner every single night* feels overwhelming and like you're not sure where to start. However, by thinking in themes—Meatless Monday, Pasta Tuesday, Soup Wednesday, New Recipe Thursday, and Takeout Friday— suddenly the meals task feels less daunting. I've narrowed the scope of the activity, and now I have some structure to help me figure out what to do. I still have creative license and maybe I can make a ramen dish on "pasta night" and mix it up. I don't have to stick to this structure all the time—maybe one Wednesday I don't feel like cooking and order takeout instead. Or maybe I have a particularly busy week and don't have the energy to try a new recipe on Thursday. But as mentioned throughout the book, implementing this schedule *to any degree* will help make my weeks of cooking dinner smoother.

You want to think of how these types of routines can benefit your work and personal life. Theming your days. Creating a weekly flow and daily flow to your schedule. And when you have something that you want to fit into your schedule—like *learning piano*—don't count on yourself to pick a good time and find a way to do it. Create a routine that helps you make room for it easily.

MAKE IT STICK

The biggest obstacle to productivity is putting something on your to-do list with no idea when you're actually going to do it.

I call these types of routines *when:then*. To create any new behavior we have to create a trigger for actually doing it, or it always stays as something we've been "meaning to do."

I've played piano for twenty years, but I had a goal of wanting to learn new songs. If I signed up for lessons, that would be something structured that I had to attend and make sure I stuck with it. But because I had taken lessons for over a decade, I didn't really need new instruction—I could easily teach myself these songs! I just needed the time, and the push, to do it. For many people that *someday* timeline never happens and turns into *I'd really like to* or *I've been meaning to*. Many times big lofty goals, creative projects, and self-care slip into those *meaning to do* categories. Those are the things that are most important to create a *when* for, especially if they've been lingering on your Main List forever.

When it came to identifying the "when" for learning new songs on the piano, I knew that evenings would be my best time to practice, because the kids were sleeping then and didn't need my attention (my piano conveniently has headphones). So next I had to find the "when" that would be my reminder to do it. I decided that every single night I put my kids to bed, *when* I walked out of my daughter's room (I put her to bed last), *then* I would walk straight to the piano. I *Swiss-cheesed* it to make it feel like something I could stick with. My only goal was to walk from her room and sit at the piano bench.

At first I just walked straight there, played a song I already knew, and left. Sometimes it was only five minutes or less. I didn't allow myself to walk downstairs and see things I could be cleaning or start a TV show. Soon it became second nature. I acted like my own assistant and set out new sheet music in the morning, hoping that would prompt Future Me (that evening) to learn something new. Once I saw the new music out, I'd sit down and learn a few measures of the piece. Some nights I'd get bored and play for ten minutes and be done. Some nights I'd look up and realize it had been an hour. My husband started to realize that I was going to do that every night, so he started to do his own thing right after our kids' bedtime, knowing that I wouldn't be ready to watch a show together or play a board game together until I was done. It really stuck as a routine and became part of the daily rhythm. The progress happened only because I originally attached the new routine to directly follow my daughter's bedtime (which I know I will be doing every night).

Results of a study published in the *European Journal of Personal Psychology* in 2009 showed that the average time it takes for a new behavior to become automatic is sixty-six days. But you may find, as I did, that with a solid *when:then* it happens much faster, because I had the same trigger (bedtime) every single night.

You can do this *when:then* exercise for anything you want to accomplish. You can make a day of the week your *when*, like Self-Care Sunday. Keeping it loose enough takes the pressure off and gives you the flexibility to do something easy (like paint your nails or take a long bath on Sunday) or bigger (eventually book one Sunday at the spa!). In the piano example, I started small by playing songs I already know and like and eventually learned to play brand-new pieces. Starting only with new music would have stopped me in my path.

In addition to using a specific day as your *when*, you can also choose a specific time, action, or trigger for your routine. Some of the other *when:then* routines I have that might inspire you:

- *When* our monthly team meeting happens: *then* I spend thirty minutes afterward to put notes in my annual review folder about what I've been working on (something I wanted to do monthly).
- *When* it's the first day of the month: *then* I give my dogs their heartworm prevention medicine.
- *When* it's Monday: *then* I do laundry for everyone in the house and dump it right on my bed so I can't go to sleep that night until it's put away.
- *When* it's the second Saturday of the month: *then* my husband and I go on a date.
- *When* I go to the grocery store: *then* I take any of my extra recycling and drop it off at the recycling center next door.
- *When* it's Wednesday evening: *then* I watch CBS's *Survivor* and paint my nails.
- *When* it's time to send my weekly update for my boss: *then* I also quickly check my *Revisit* email folder to see if I'm missing anything from the week.
- *When* there are five minutes until dinner is ready: *then* I set a five-minute timer and tell my kids to clean up their toys and books before dinner.
- *When* it's Thursday, after my daughter's nap: *then* I leave out something creative or artistic for her to do so those craft supplies get used!
- *When* it's Friday night: *then* we have pizza and play a family board game or watch a family movie.

- *When* I brush my teeth every night: *then* I do anything else that I want to do daily, like take a vitamin or repeat daily affirmations.
- *When* it's Tuesday: *then* my family and I participate in a no-technology routine from dinner to bed (more on No Tech Tuesday in Chapter 18).
- *When* it's July 4 or New Year's: *then* I do anything I want to do every six months like replace filters in my house, replace mascara, wash couch cushions, and a whole bunch of other things. (I have a big six-month list.)
- *When* it's my birthday week: *then* I schedule any annual doctor appointments I need, like an eye exam or physical.

Routines get things off your plate and out of your brain because you've reserved an exact time and place for them later. I could be haunted by needing to *wash my outdoor couch cushions sometime*, all the time. Instead, I use minimal energy points and think of it only twice a year because I've set an exact time for it every six months and I trust my system. I don't catch myself wondering, *When was my last eye exam?* I know it was last December because it's always the week of my birthday. These cadences and routines stick—and they make life easier and more enjoyable.

MEMORY ATTACHMENTS

You can also use *when:then* association as a single-instance mnemonic device. Let's say I'm lying in bed at night before I leave for a trip, and I remember something I forgot to pack. I envision myself doing something I *know* I will do in the morning, and then immediately envision that version of Future Me remembering what I need. Think, *When I grab the keys off the hook, then remember I need my phone charger*, three or more times. The next morning when I go to grab my keys, that association has been made so effectively that the image of my phone charger pops into my head. Attaching something to something else ensures that it doesn't get forgotten. I came up with this as a way to remember things when I couldn't access my Capture list and now it's something I use almost daily and have taught others.

Another way to use *when:then* is when deciding where to place things in your home or organizational system. Let's say you're not sure where to store your tape in your house. Imagine that item was lost; the first place it pops into your mind to look for it is where you should store it in the first place. So imagine your roommate said to you, *Hey, I can't find the tape, do you know where it is?* What is the first place that pops to your mind to go check for it? That should be the place you store it! You're first testing the *when I need the tape, then I look here* connection your brain has already made and then using it to your advantage to put it in its natural place.

TAKE ADVANTAGE OF NATURAL STARTS

In addition to grouping things that happen daily, weekly, monthly, annually together to make life easier, you can take advantage of beginnings, too. In *When: The Scientific Secrets of Perfect Timing*, Daniel Pink talks about avoiding false starts by using the power of temporal landmarks for making fresh starts. Like Monday, the first day of the week, the first of a month, the first day on the new job, or a new year. Our brains are wired to think of these as new beginnings. We want to take advantage of that. You are much more likely to stick with a routine if you start it on a Monday instead of a Thursday or Friday.

Making routines and using the *when:then* model removes the stress and anxiety of remembering to perform tasks before we've even done them. It helps us find the actual time and space to accomplish those "one day" things we've been wanting to do. When there is more of a routine and cadence, there is less distraction, and more mental space for doing the things we want and need to do. But, as we noted in Chapter 16, as long as there are computers and other digital devices in our world (and there always will be), stress and distraction are always waiting at the door.

Taking small periods of time away from these devices can be one of the healthiest things we do for ourselves and one of the best ways to reboot our Uptime.

PRODUCTIVITY PRACTICES

- Find something you've been meaning to do "someday" but keeps getting neglected or pushed off until some vague future date. Attach it to another activity on the same schedule and create a routine for it.
- Use the power of *when:then* associations to commit things to memory, find a natural home for things, and inspire actions.
- Find some natural new starts in the calendar—like the first day of the month or your birthday—to begin new routines, giving them a better chance of sticking.

Chapter

18

NO-TECH TUESDAY

If you've heard of FOMO you know it means: the fear of missing out. But increasingly popular recently is JOMO: the *joy* of missing out. The idea is that sometimes we are actually even happier when we miss that email, text, podcast, or plans we didn't really want to follow through on. In a blog post on the *Psychology Today* website, Kristen Fuller, MD, wrote that "JOMO allows us to be who we are in the present moment, which is the secret to finding happiness. When you free up that competitive and anxious space in your brain, you have so much more time, energy and emotion to conquer your true priorities."

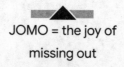

JOMO = the joy of
missing out

As mentioned throughout this book, *the quiet mind is where the magic happens.* It's where new ideas are created, old ideas are restructured, energy points are gained, and information is absorbed and processed. All our noisy devices have intruded on much of that quiet time. Hundreds of years ago humans would accomplish daylong journeys on horseback with nothing to distract them besides views of nature, the open air, and the company of others. Today we can barely get through a dinner with a friend without picking up our phone.

I truly believe that the journey to a more intentional, productive life starts with an examination of your relationship with technology. Are you giving yourself an hour of mental silence a day? Or are you cramming every down moment with a quick check of social media or the news? Are you waking up to your day, or waking up to your email? Are you spending time with your own kids only to catch yourself watching a social media video of someone else's kids? Technology is certainly helpful and bridges so many gaps in our lives, but it's important to take a look at how it can work *for* you instead of *against* you.

THE CHALLENGE

I'm not one for radical New Year's resolutions (I believe small changes over time are more effective), but a while back my husband and I decided we would start the new year by making a small change: try to put away devices between dinner and bedtime one night a week. We started our own No-Tech Tuesday Night, where we'd find activities outside of technology like board games, puzzles, spending time outdoors, or new creative hobbies.

Because the exercise required minimal commitment, was easy to keep up with, and ended up being fun and relaxing, we stuck with it for an entire year. Those Tuesdays ended up being some of our favorite nights. Technology is so beneficial in helping us work, bringing us together with others, and facilitating ways to accomplish more. But even for computers running in uptime, rebooting and powering down occasionally are crucial to long-term operational success. The same is true of our Uptime—one night a week powering down without devices reboots our brains, gives us more energy points, and sets us up for long-term productivity success. By practicing the JOMO ideology just one night a week, you make room for richer in-person connections, deeper reflection during alone time, better sleep, and a more refreshed morning the following day.

My own success with this weekly tradition made me want to lead a similar effort with others at Google. I took some of my own advice from the last few chapters. I knew that if I wanted to start a movement it needed to begin with:

- A *small change*: Hardly anyone wants a total overhaul, like turning in their smartphone for a flip phone. I had to Swiss-cheese it and decided to focus on a manageable and achievable goal, like turning off the phone for a few hours.
- A *when:then routine*: *Pick one night a week* is so much less powerful than *No-Tech Tuesday*. It's catchy; it gives direction, rhythm, and structure. *When* it's Tuesday, *then* I do something other than tech that evening. I chose Tuesday night, mostly because *Tech* and *Tuesday* both start with a *T*!
- A *natural start*: The middle of July might feel random to start an initiative like this, but the beginning of the year could feel more natural. People are usually evaluating their productivity and willing to make a bigger change since it's the start of something *new*. I decided the challenge would begin in January.

These insights led me to start the annual *No-Tech Tuesday Night* challenge at Google: on Tuesdays in January and February (or one other night of the week of your choosing), give up digital devices and screens just from dinner to bedtime. For the last five years over 2,500 people have accepted the challenge annually, and the results have been amazing.

Almost all the feedback I hear is that it's hard at first—but worth it in the end. Over the past five years, key feedback themes include comments that participants:

- Are surprised by the number of times they go to pick up and check their phone
- Can't believe how much more time they seem to have that evening
- Sleep much better at night
- Have richer human connections that wouldn't have happened when technology was present
- Are encouraged by how much teammates/managers/colleagues/ friends were not only supportive but joined in
- Find themselves much more energetic the next day
- Finally find time for creative hobbies
- See that by putting aside a problem they need to work on for one night, it actually results in better solutions the following day
- Realize that their families, especially children, love it
- Plan to incorporate it long term or expand on the challenge

At the end of the challenge each year I posit two important true/false questions, and you can see the results for yourself:

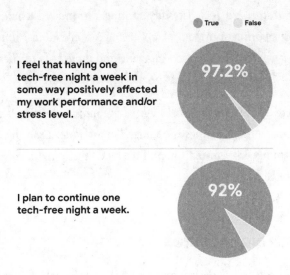

I was overjoyed, but not surprised, to find that those participating in the challenge reported that it had made a difference in their overall stress, well-being, and performance, and that the majority of them planned to continue it. Some participants have been doing the challenge for five years and have kept up with every single Tuesday night since the first year I held it.

While the quantitative feedback speaks volumes, the qualitative feedback says even more. Some of my favorite quotes:

> After four weeks in, I finally understood what the author of Winnie the Pooh meant by "Doing nothing often leads to the very best of something."

> My sleep improved, got great ideas and inspiration and feel amazing. Tuesday is my new favorite day! :)

> This challenge also provided an opportunity for self-reflection. It made me realize how much time I spend on my devices and how easy it is to get caught up in the never-ending cycle of scrolling, refreshing, and checking notifications.

> I was working on a work problem I was trying to solve when the alarm went off to start No Tech Tuesday evening. Normally I would have spent hours poring over the problem trying to solve it but I unplugged instead. I woke up Wednesday morning and thought of the best solution—I'm convinced it was because I let my brain rest.

> Unexpectedly my kids love it. I realized the main reason they are on their devices in the evenings is because I'm on mine. I sat and did a puzzle with my 13-year-old son and we had a meaningful conversation, which can be rare these days.

TEN TIPS FOR DIGITAL DETOX

Maybe a full tech-free evening still feels like too much commitment to you. That's okay. You can Swiss-cheese it even further and just find small habits throughout your week or day to feel some of these deeper connections and moments of clarity. Here are ten of my favorite tips for taking small steps for digital detox:

1. **Put your phone to bed, ideally at least an hour before your bedtime.** Stick to it and set an alarm to remember to put your phone away, maybe on its charger.

2. **Give your phone a bedroom outside of your bedroom.** Put it on loud if you need to hear it for emergencies. If you can't put it outside your room, at least put it *across* the room so you have to make an extra effort to retrieve it.

3. **Try to do *one* thing before picking your phone up in the morning.** Make your coffee, take your shower, or get dressed before you touch your phone.

4. **Find short windows of time to leave your phone behind.** Leave it behind just while you go on a short walk, while you put your kids to bed, or just while you eat lunch. Whatever you can do to give your brain clear moments to give the other things you need to think about time to "seep in" to your brain.

5. **The crowding-out method:** Tell yourself you have to do something for fifteen minutes *before* engaging with tech in the evenings. For example, tell yourself on weeknights, before you watch TV, that you have to knit for fifteen minutes. Keep it short enough that it feels easy to stick with.

6. **Turn your background image on your phone or computer to something neutral,** such as a picture of grass or a solid white background. Why? Because it's boring to pick up an empty blue screen. There's less of a *jolt* of happiness to experience versus when you see that cute picture of your dog. Going further, you can set your phone to grayscale, which also reduces the temptation to pick it up.

7. **Trade phones with your spouse/partner/roommate** while you watch TV or eat dinner. Have you ever checked someone else's social media or email? It's boring.

8. **Delete social media and news apps on your phone** and only view them on your computer. Making them slightly less accessible will prevent you from using them out of habit, and having to scroll with your mouse instead of your thumb makes them less enticing. Alternatively you can set a schedule on your mobile device of when you're able to access them or impose time limits.

9. **Use the currency method:** Earn a minute of screen time for every minute spent outside (our pediatrician insists on this for kids in her book*!). Tell yourself you need to be outside for an hour first to earn an hour of TV.

10. **Consider some of these other things to help reduce your dependence on your phone:** get an old-fashioned alarm clock, use a home phone, or get a lockbox for your phone that unlocks only with a timer for the phone's "bedtime."

Digital detoxing—even just that one evening each week—creates the mental space we need to thrive in our work and in our lives and to connect socially and emotionally with our colleagues, our families, and ourselves. It lifts the brain fog and provides a much-needed reboot, preventing burnout and fostering Uptime. You may find that once you've taken these small steps, you can make bigger moves away from devices in even more dramatic ways throughout the week and that when you are using your devices, you're using them in a better, more intentional way. As we have seen, even the smallest change can make a big difference. Another one of those small changes you can make is starting your morning in a different way to control the direction of your day.

---

* https://www.amazon.com/Healthy-Kids-Unhealthy-World-Practical/dp/1735622222 /ref=sr_1_1?hvadid=676936605963&hvdev=c&hvlocphy=9009996&hvnetw=g &hvqmt=e&hvrand=15082042399793829514&hvtargid=kwd-1457583165041& hydadcr=22132_13517543&keywords=healthy+kids+in+an+unhealthy+world&qid=169 7477434&sr=8-1

PRODUCTIVITY PRACTICES

- Pick a night of the week that feels doable and give up technology from dinner to bedtime. See what happens, and take note of the benefits.
- Find small times throughout the day to unplug. As these unplugged moments become regular, ask yourself if you have changed your overall habits when it comes to technology.

MINDFUL MORNINGS

After the success of the No-Tech Tuesday challenge, I decided to add a component: Wake Up Wednesday. It was rooted in the idea that you could ride the wave of your peaceful, technologically disconnected evening (followed by great sleep) through an additional hour the following morning. Starting your morning with thirty minutes to an hour of doing something *you* want to do, without plugging into technology, can help set you up for a great day. It ensures you've done something for yourself before you do anything else. This one simple routine gives you more energy points to use the rest of the day.

I call these first thirty minutes of my day the "Laura 30." I wake up before the rest of my family and do whatever I want, for half an hour, without using devices. Usually I start with meditation. Then, sometimes I read, sometimes I play piano with headphones on, sometimes I look at affirmation cards or write in my journal. Sometimes I get a workout in if I know I won't be able to for the rest of the day. The point is that the thirty minutes are the routine. They are my time to do what I want before I spend the rest of the day doing what everyone else wants. I don't always plan what I'm doing ahead of time. I decide that morning on whatever I'm in the mood for.

One thirty-minute block affects my whole day and keeps me from feeling like I barrel-rolled out of bed, checked my email, and slid into mom mode followed by work mode followed by mom mode again. Even if I do all of those other things, I take some comfort knowing that I started with myself first—filling my own cup before pouring my energy into everyone else's. Cutting my evening short thirty minutes earlier to go to bed and make room for this in my schedule the next morning does not make much difference in my evening. However, doing so allows me to wake up and have those uninterrupted thirty minutes the next morning, which makes a huge difference in my day. Those same thirty minutes on the opposite side of my sleep schedule make an immediate, positive impact on my day.

Here is some of the best feedback about Wake Up Wednesday I received when I gave this challenge to my Google colleagues:

> I love No-Tech Tuesday—Wake Up Wednesday proved even better. I tend to read the news and catch up on notifications first thing in the morning. Not staring at my phone immediately seems to be giving me an extra bit of focus throughout the day.

> I realized that I spent a lot of time in the mornings (right after I get up) just handling notifications and browsing social media on my phone or looking at emails that can wait. Without this to distract me on Wake Up Wednesdays, I find that my morning routine has been faster and I get to work with a fresher mindset!

START YOUR DAY BEFORE YOU NEED TO

Even if you're not a morning person, I urge you to start your day before you think you have to. Don't let your first commitment of the day be your

When you get control of your morning,
you get control of your day.

alarm. Start your day on your own terms. The kids, a conference call, a dog that needs to be walked—those aren't the things that should wake you up. Wake up to find time for yourself, even if it's just fifteen minutes before the kids, the dog, and the conference call beckon.

Mornings don't have to be about productivity or getting something huge done. Sundar Pichai, CEO of Google, has a surprisingly simple morning routine that includes an omelet and toast, a cup of tea, and reading a physical newspaper every day. What you're actually doing in the morning is less important than the act of starting your day with purpose and consistency.

There is a reason that you hear that some of the most successful people start their days early. You don't have to start at 5:00 a.m., but if you go to bed a little earlier and start your day before your first commitment, you're more likely to accomplish something that matters to you before the day begins. I don't know anyone who sets their alarm to wake up early and play video games, scroll social media, or binge-watch a TV show before work, but staying up late is usually filled with activities like this. Find the sweet spot of going with your natural rhythms to make the most of your mornings.

Know that changes to your sleep schedule can take time to be absorbed. If waking up earlier feels daunting, Swiss-cheese it and commit to waking up just five minutes earlier for a few days. Maybe you increase it after seeing the benefits of five quiet minutes. Consider doing a one-week test of waking up to your own thirty-minute activity. At the end of a week note how you feel and ask yourself if it's worth sticking with. Pick something to do in the first thirty minutes of your day that makes waking up worth it. For me, it's time alone. For my husband, it's a cinnamon roll or reading the *Wall Street Journal* uninterrupted.

THE MORNING THREE

In addition to giving yourself a little extra time in the morning, I recommend three things that will help set you up for a focused and satisfying day.

1. **Music:** Music sets the mood; it's the tone or the "background feeling" that we don't even notice consciously sometimes. Ever been at a gathering or party that feels a little awkward? I can guarantee there isn't any music on or the music isn't right for the vibe. My time as an event planner taught me that the right music makes or breaks the mood. Make a feel-good morning and relaxing playlist that you put on as you're eating breakfast or getting dressed. Use a smart device to set a routine and have it start playing automatically. When my kids come down for breakfast, instrumental Disney music is playing in our kitchen.

2. **Lighting:** Nothing triggers our early morning brains to stress more than bright or intense lighting, which is why staying off your devices for the first few minutes of the day can make a huge difference, as can adjusting the lighting in your home. Try dimming your lights or turning on just lamps instead of your overhead lights. In my house I have just our undercabinet lighting on in the kitchen and I open the curtains in my children's room first to wake them up with natural light. I even use an alarm clock that slowly gets brighter as it approaches my wake time to mimic the natural rising of the sun.

3. **A Gift for Future You:** Nothing is more delightful than waking up and realizing that Past You did something to set up Future You for a pleasant and stress-free morning. There's nothing like waking up and remembering that you already emptied the dishwasher last night, already made those school lunches, or you already packed your bag for work or picked out your outfit. That feeling of something *already being done* is so wonderful. I try to have one thing delightfully ready when my kids come downstairs, like an invitation to their day.

This could be breakfast already done, their cup of milk out, or even sometimes a coloring page with some crayons to play with while I cook breakfast. I know they feel good when they're greeted in the morning by something that's already been set out for them and I feel the same. For me, that's setting the timer for coffee the night before so that it's already ready to go when I get up that morning. Not to mention that the smell of coffee helps trigger my brain to wake up faster (a great example of the *state dependency* we discussed in Chapter 10). Such a delight!

POWER OF MEDITATION

If someone stopped me on the street and asked me to name one thing they could do to be more productive, I wouldn't say anything about lists or time management. I would say find time to meditate, every single day. *Why does spending ten minutes doing nothing help you do everything?* Because regular meditation can:

- Lower blood pressure
- Increase mental clarity and focus
- Increase performance
- Provide stress relief
- Improve sleep
- Reduce anxiety and memory loss
- Increase attention span

All of that could be accomplished by the same activity—for just ten minutes daily!

Meditation is sometimes regarded as something people can do to be *peaceful*, which is certainly true. However, it's important to note that it's also a straight-up mental workout. It's mental hygiene, just like brushing your teeth is dental hygiene. It's finding the quiet space *between* thoughts. It's the fastest way to focus and a *train-your-brain* shortcut. It's

"If you don't have time to meditate for ten minutes, you should meditate for twenty."
—Zen proverb

lifting *above* the fog instead of trying to power through. It's sharpening the knife before you cut one hundred sweet potatoes. Most importantly, it's the fastest way for your brain to access a productive Uptime state. And it takes only ten minutes a day.

When we don't have time for meditation is often just when we need it the most. Taking ten minutes to meditate will make that hourlong work block feel like you got two hours' worth of work done. It will stretch out those moments of time with your loved ones and let you really enjoy them. I woke up early on my wedding day to meditate because I wanted to start with mental clarity as I experienced one of the best days of my life. (My hair and makeup person was a little mad because I was ten minutes late, but it was worth it.) As my meditation practice has grown more consistent, I have experienced a considerable difference in how my day flows and the type of thoughts that pop into my head. Even if I have to leave by 5:00 a.m. to catch a flight, I still make sure to get that meditation time in because I know how much it affects my day.

The benefit of meditation, like time at the gym, takes a while to build. After one day you won't necessarily feel the results but you likely will start to after ten days. After a month you will certainly feel different. To get started you have to Swiss-cheese and find the starting place that feels doable. If ten minutes a day feels overwhelming, how about two minutes a day? (You never know—you might end up sitting for ten!) The type of meditation doesn't matter. Guided meditation. Mindfulness meditation. Meditation music. There are books, apps, and online videos to help you start. It can be as simple as sitting in actual silence for ten minutes and listening gently to your air conditioning unit. I like the sound of a river flowing. It's the act of focusing on not focusing that's important.

Just like different types of workouts, find a meditation approach you like and you'll be far more likely to stick with it.

A regular meditation practice allows you to feel more present, helps to create more space between the moments of your day, and brings out the small details of each experience. For example, at work you may be surprised to find yourself very focused during a meeting (without having to "childproof" and close all your tabs), being less stressed about an upcoming deadline or particularly large to-do list, having more creative ideas and/or sharper mental clarity, all as a result of a regular meditation practice. I convinced one colleague of mine to start meditation and after two to three weeks of daily practice he told me that the same cloudiness/business of work was there, but he had just slightly "risen above" the clouds so he was less affected by them and could see it all more clearly with a new view.

ATTENTION TRAINING

Sometimes people find that certain activities create a meditative-like state and those types of activities can be helpful *in addition to* meditation. This is similar to going to the gym (meditation) but then *also* living an active life (taking your dog on a walk, going on hikes, cycling, taking the stairs). Activities as simple as knitting, playing a musical instrument, reading a book, or doing a puzzle are still active times for your brain and help increase that focus muscle. They may not be quite as powerful as the time spent focusing on *nothing* (meditation), but many find that adjacent activities that are attention focusers help increase mental clarity.

I host a reading challenge every year (*One-Book-A-Week*) that invites Googlers to read at the pace of about a book every week for one quarter. I started it after finding that this is a habit that some of the world's most productive people adopt. Regular reading is good for attention training, being exposed to new ideas, and creating brain space. One study showed that as little as six minutes of reading each day can reduce a person's stress level by 68 percent, helping to clear the mind and minimize body tension.

Many participants say the weeks of the reading challenge end up being their most productive time of the year—in all aspects of their lives. That is ironic given that they are adding *more* to their plate by committing to read a book each week. It's because they are more focused overall, more deliberate about scheduling their time to get it done, they are sharpening their brain's focus muscle when reading, and they've used the crowding-out method of less social media or TV or extra work because they need to spend that time reading. This is a great example of how productivity and well-being go hand in hand. To perform at your best and make the biggest impact, you need to be well rested and well nourished, and give your brain a chance to relax into different activities, like reading.

TAKE THE MORNING MAGIC WITH YOU

Even if you haven't found time yet for a morning "You 30" routine, here are some ways you can find moments—even a second or less—of mindfulness throughout the day and mimic that magic that comes with a peaceful morning.

- Close your eyes and savor that first sip of a hot beverage.
- Be fully present for the last moment of a hot shower before you step out.
- Turn off the music/radio/podcast in your car for the last minute of your morning drive and envision how your day would look if everything went perfectly.
- Make true eye contact with anyone you're talking to or interacting with (you should know the eye color of the person who took your order!).
- Eat one meal or snack alone with no devices and practice really focusing on the sensation of your taste buds.
- Use the "teeth brushing" cadence or daily "bookend" for moments with spouses/children/roommates. Really focus on being present for the first greeting of the day and the last moment with them that day.

- Soak up any moment you're in a hug and never be the one to let go first (I do this with my kids!).
- Listen to an entire album or entire song instead of pressing next immediately (you'll forget how much you love the whole thing).
- Practice gratitude using the *when:then* pattern for something you already have to do. *When* I put on my shoes, *then* I think of one thing I'm grateful for. *When* I'm washing my hands, *then* I try to feel the water on my hands and ground myself in the present moment.
- When you're rushing out the door and leaving the house for the day, stop in the frame of the door and take a huge deep breath, grounding yourself in the moment and preparing to pivot to the rest of the day. (If you leave as a group with a partner/spouse/family, maybe hold hands and do it together!)

All of these small steps become routines that help bring peace, gratitude, and mindfulness to your day. It doesn't have to be something huge or time-consuming. These morning routines and mindfulness practices, paired with digital detox, help you become productive and achieve Uptime easier.

So, how do we know when we've "made it"?

PRODUCTIVITY PRACTICES

- Carve out a "You 30" time block in the morning and decide each morning what you'd like to do with it. Do whatever you're in the mood for that day!
- Set up a daily meditation practice—start small and make it easy.
- Start your morning with relaxing music, soft lighting, and something delightfully done.
- Find a few moments throughout the day to practice mindfulness for mental clarity and make them routines.

Chapter

20

ACHIEVING UPTIME

By now, you've decided *what* to focus on, you know *when* to do it, you've mastered *where* to work, and you know *how* to do it all well. You've also set up mental best practices to live well *while* doing it.

Successful, prosperous people *do* use their time more deliberately than the average person—and now you have the tools to do the same. In fact, it becomes easier and easier because you're accomplishing things in a way that feels natural and "with the flow." You're using fewer energy points to do the same things because you're floating downstream. Being productive doesn't have to be difficult. You can be busy with all the right things and flow through your day both happy and completely on top of things in Uptime.

SMALL CHANGES, BIG IMPACT

The important thing to remember is that implementing these tips *to any degree* will make a change in your life and work. If you can set only one boundary, if you have just one hot spot, if you make a calendar

▲

**Direction is more important
than speed.**

---

template and it works only 50 percent of the time—any of those changes will help you *feel* a difference.

Imagine a car in the center of a circle. The car is you and your work, and your goal is to get to the circle's perimeter in Uptime. If you turn the steering wheel just a tiny bit in either direction, and send the car straight, it will end up at a radically different point on the outside of the circle. This—your aim, your course, your *intention*—is far more important than how fast you're working, how much you're getting done or churning out. Making sure you steer that car in the right way is so much more important to where you end up than how quickly you got there. That's how you can think of these changes, tiny steering adjustments. Setting priorities allows you to focus on what's important. Learning your own energy rhythms allows you to work when and where you work best. And while meditating for ten minutes may seem like a small daily change, it will steady your speed and give you complete control of your overall direction.

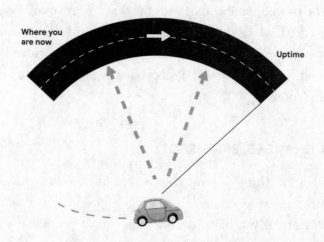

WHAT'S NEXT?

You might be excited by all the information in this book but wondering where to start. Maybe you read the whole book in a day, and now you're wondering what tomorrow looks like. Or you're wondering how to gradually start implementing these practices into your work life. At the end of my trainings I give people a few moments to write down three things that really stuck out to them and I urge you to do the same. If a friend stopped you on the street right now and asked you three things you learned from this book, what would they be?

These are the best places to start—with the things that resonated and that your brain has already brought into memory! So much of the Productivity Practices and getting to Uptime is using the brain's strengths—and understanding its weaknesses—to maximize your effectiveness.

Some people feel like they love their own list system but need help with an overload of meetings. Some people love the Daily List format but don't need as much help with finding downtime. Others are intrigued by the concept of meditation and mindful mornings. Your brain has already mentally highlighted the parts of this book you need most; trust it and start there. Maybe flip to the chapter that stuck out to you most and start with those Productivity Practices listed at the end.

I encourage you to use this guide like a recipe book (following specific sets of instructions in order) or a sushi menu (mixing and matching different sections to find a combination that's just right for you). But always start with what you're most excited about! And remember that implementing these practices *to any degree* will reap benefits in your work and personal life.

HOW TO MEASURE PRODUCTIVITY

People often ask me, *How do you measure productivity? How do I know I'm productive?* In a business, we can look at outputs, such as number of outbound calls, revenue goals, employee retention, or amount of code written. However, when it comes to personal productivity, the best indicator of success is *how you feel*. You can regularly ask yourself: *Do I feel rejuvenated? Am I on top of my work? Am I feeling creative? Present? Balanced? Energized?* If you're answering yes, that's Uptime.

Wherever you find yourself right now, there is always a way to move toward your Uptime. With a full-time job, and three kids under the age of four, there are certainly times I feel stressed and overwhelmed, or times that things don't go as exactly as I planned (like my son being born a month early, right when I was scheduled to finish writing this book)! When those unexpected things happen, I give myself grace, and then get myself back on track using the exact methods I've outlined in these chapters. My hope is that the tools and techniques in this book will give you the same sense of confidence in your ability to get things done and to live well while doing them.

So many of the people I've trained or individually coached email me afterward to share that they are happier, working more effectively, and living with more clarity, and that's my favorite part. Those testimonies are what it means to have mastered *Uptime*. It's your life, talent, interests, intentions, and priorities seamlessly executed while finding well-being for yourself. It's holistic accomplishment in all areas of your life. You have the tools—now what will you do with them?

ACKNOWLEDGMENTS

First, I'd like to thank God for giving me this gift, Sundar for helping me recognize it, and Googlers for letting it grow (the over 55,000 of you on my Weekly Tips list and so many of you who have supported and encouraged me throughout the years). This book and my program would not exist without all of you!

To Bruce and Dom, thank you for countless hours poring over this text, all of your honesty, input, and feedback to shape this book into what it is. Thank you, Bruce, for managing my exclamation points and emoticon usage to a reasonable level :), and for giving Dom and me the outside perspective we needed. Thank you, Dom, for coming up with the title, for teaching me what my own voice sounds like in writing, and then helping me give it wings—you have made a huge impact on my life and I look up to you as an author!

To Ma'ayan, thank you for beautifully bringing to images what was in my mind and in the text. Your cover design and creativity in each chapter have contributed greatly to the end product of this book—not to mention your work with my program over the last eight years! Thank you to my agent, Jim Levine, for guiding me as a first-time author and for living out my teachings before I even wrote about them. (Thanks to Jonathan and Alan for your support and for introducing me to him!) Thank you to Hollis (and Kirby!) for believing in my book from the start and trusting me throughout the process; it made me trust myself!

To the Chicago Badmins (Tracy, Barb, Cadi, and Kate), thank you for being the first five people to join my newsletter and supporting me from the very beginning. Thanks to Kaisa Holden for convincing me to make a g2g course about Inbox Management and to Robert Kyncel and Jim Lecinski for first believing in my executive work. Thanks to Karen Sauder for being my first shining example of what it means to be a great mom and an executive woman. Thanks to Alison Wagonfield for sponsoring my book and guiding me throughout the entire process. Thank you to James Freedman, Marc Ellenbogen, Katie Wattie, and Emily Singer for reading and countless others for your reviews and support internally. Thanks to Jenny Wood for entering the world of authorhood with me—I couldn't have done it without you! To Neil and Gopi for all of your advice. Thanks to Chadwords for being the Class Hotel person I know will always have time to talk to me, and for teaching me how to use my time *wisely* at work. Thanks to Kyle Moncelle (and Josh!) for being the kind of friends that stick and for sharing my love of all things books. Thanks to Kate Kolbert-Hyle for being a mentor, friend, and professional woman I look up to so much. Thanks to Jess Kohen for your support and being the person I discuss all the things with and Sca for being there since the beginning. Thanks to Mark, Filipe, and Lanaeschia for reminding me how great it can be to work with a team and reminding me that collaboration does matter. Thanks to the Mama Bear Book Club and Time Travelers Wives (Michelle, Beth, Sarah, and Summer) for listening to my month-by-month updates, helping me brainstorm titles, and giving me five years of murder mysteries and enjoyable conversation—I hope my book passes our Goodreads review test!!!

Thanks to Tom Oliveri for being a wonderful manager and, more importantly, a caring person. Thank you for both the freedom and structure to grow and for being my "biggest loser" email success story. Thanks to Anas for teaching me how to be assertive, how to value my time, how to prioritize family in a business environment, showing me my potential before I saw it, and for supporting me countless ways over the years—you are the most influential mentor I've ever had. Thanks to Dave Moerlein and Lindsey Schultz, the best first managers anyone could ever ask for, both of whom encouraged (and modeled!) to me to do what I'm good at *and* passionate about, and never, ever settle for less.

Thanks to Margo for teaching me that having lollipops in your purse is the magical key to motherhood and that planning and organization is not what makes a house a home, but it certainly helps :). Thanks to Mrs. Herbster for showing me that creating wonderful experiences for others starts with printing things on neon paper and putting them in plastic folders (plus a whole lot of support and love!)—you already know, but you changed my life! Thanks to DECA for teaching me professionalism and etiquette and to POB for teaching me (way before I believed you) that lipstick really is the finishing touch. And eternal gratitude to Ester Hicks, my favorite author and speaker who inspires much of what I do and write.

Thanks to Michele for being good at literally everything that anyone could possibly need help with and using so many of those superpowers to help me. The best Tita, friend, sister, writer, cook, camp counselor, co-worker, babysitter, floral arranger, baker, PP doula, color analyzer, the list goes on. And thanks for editing the book. But not just editing, adding value. See what I did there? Do you? Thanks for telling me the real truth about the text that everyone else was thinking but not saying. You're a true co-author and deserve the credit. And thanks to the weekly tip team (Jake Gordan and Paul Teresi), for being the small but mighty group that supports my newsletter.

Thanks to my parents for raising me to believe I could do whatever I wanted to do, and supporting me for the entire ride. Thanks Moom for taking Ford on stroller walks so I could finish writing and to Faj for making our childhood *Another Day in Paradise* and for telling me this was the best book you've read in ten years! (It's the only book you've read in ten years . . .) Thanks to Leigh and D Sal for always believing in me (like that time I definitely did have a cough drop and you believed me). Thanks to Pam and Bob for such support for our kiddos and for letting me write the first part of this book at your dining room table.

To Marie, thank you for teaching me that time management before a child and time management after a child are ENTIRELY different beasts—you rocked our world in the best way possible and you continue to light it up every day. To Xavier, thank you for teaching me what pure joy looks like and for requesting I stop singing to you when I'm putting you to bed, which actually helped me remember how special silence can be. Thanks to Ford for reminding me that not even the best planners can plan when babies come, you and I did this book together. Being a mom to you three is the best job I will ever have.

And to my husband, Jake, thank you for being my number one fan. You're a pillar of both my productivity and my well-being. You're also the smartest person I know. Thank you for talking me off a ledge when my water broke and the book was not close to finished. Thank you for taking care of anything I needed so I could finish it. Thanks for being my first reader and my best friend. I feel lucky that I got to publish a book, but that pales in comparison to how lucky I feel to have the beautiful life we've built together.

NOTES

xviii The results of a study: Joseph S. Reiff, Hal E. Hershfield, and Jordi Quoidbach, "Identity Over Time: Perceived Similarity Between Selves Predicts Well-Being 10 Years Later," *Social Psychological and Personality Science* 11, no. 2 (2020): 160–67.

3 A 2018 study at Ohio University: Arkady Konovalov and Ian Krajbich, "Neurocomputational Dynamics of Sequence Learning," *Neuron* 98, no. 6 (2018): 1282–93.

9 "Eisenhower method": Mind Tools Content Team, "Eisenhower's Urgent/ Important Principle: Using Time Effectively, Not Just Efficiently," https:// www.mindtools.com/al1e0k5/eisenhowers-urgentimportant-principle.

10 Eisenhower's 1954 remark: Dwight D. Eisenhower, Address at the Second Assembly of the World Council of Churches, Evanston, IL, American Presidency Project, https://www.presidency.ucsb.edu/node/232572.

28 A renowned study: Sarah Gardner and Dave Albee, "Study Focuses on Strategies for Achieving Goals, Resolutions," press release 266, Dominican University of California, February 2015.

29 "will save you up to two hours": Brian Tracy, *Eat That Frog!* (Oakland: Berrett-Koehler, 2017), chap. 2.

36 most difficult/important task first: Tracy, *Eat That Frog!*, introduction.

48 a 2016 study: David A. Kalmbach et al., "Genetic Basis of Chronotype in Humans: Insights from Three Landmark GWAS," *Sleep* 40 (2017).

51 According to research: Mareike B. Wieth and Rose T. Zacks, "Time of Day Effects on Problem Solving: When the Non-Optimal is Optimal," *Thinking and Reasoning* 17, no. 4 (2011): 387–401.

57 Business leaders, including: Web Desk, "Find Out the Daily Routines That Drive 40 Successful Business Leaders," Digital Information World, May 25, 2021, https://www.digitalinformationworld.com/2021/05/the -work-routines-of-musk-branson-dorsey-37-other-business-leaders.html.

57 A study in the *Journal of Experimental Psychology*: Joshua S. Rubenstein, David E. Meyer, and Jeffrey E. Evans, "Executive Control of Cognitive Processes in Task Switching," *Journal of Experimental Psychology: Human Perception and Performance* 27, no. 4 (2001): 763–97.

74 Timothy A. Pychyl: Timothy A. Pychl, *Solving the Procrastination Puzzle* (New York: Tarcher/Penguin, 2014).

74 seven attributes of a task: Chris Bailey, "Here's Why You Procrastinate, and 10 Tactics That Will Help You Stop," interview, ChrisBailey.com, March 27, 2014, https://chrisbailey.com/why-you-procrastinate-10-tactics -to-help-you-stop/.

86 *The Montessori Baby*: Simone Davies and Junnifa Uzodike, *The Montessori Baby* (New York: Workman, 2021), chap. 5.

86 A great deal of research: Shahram Heshmat, PhD, "5 Benefits of Boredom," *Science of Choice* (blog), *Psychology Today*, April 4, 2020, https:// www.psychologytoday.com/us/blog/science-choice/202004/5-benefits -boredom.

86 double-blind study: Sandi Mann and Rebekah Cadman, "Does Being Bored Make Us More Creative?," *Creativity Research Journal* 26, no. 2 (2014): 165–73.

99 two groups of deep-sea divers: Jaap M. J. Murre, "The Godden and Baddeley (1975) Experiment on Context-Dependent Memory on Land and Underwater: A Replication," *Royal Society Open Science* 8, no. 11 (2021).

126 *Harvard Business Review* survey: Leslie A. Perlow, Constance Noonan Hadley, and Eunice Eun, "Stop the Meeting Madness," *Harvard Business Review*, July–August 2017, 62–69.

126 An article in: Steven G. Rogelberg, Cliff Scott, and John Kello, "The Science and Fiction of Meetings," MIT *Sloan Management Review*, December 2007, 18–21.

126 a 2010 study: Steven Rogelberg, Joseph Allen, Linda Shanock, Cliff Scott, and Marissa Shuffle, "Employee Satisfaction with Meetings: A

Contemporary Facet of Job Satisfaction," *Human Resource Management*, March 2010, 149–72.

128   one of my favorite productivity books: Cameron Herold, *Meetings Suck* (Austin, TX: Lioncrest, 2016), chap. 5.

131   once you have seven people in a meeting: Marcia W. Blenko, Michael C. Mankins, and Paul Rogers, *Decide & Deliver* (Boston: Harvard Business Review Press, 2010), chap. 4.

143   A calculation by the education platform Brainscape: Andrew Cohen, "How Keyboard Shortcuts Could Revive America's Economy," Brainscape, n.d., https://www.brainscape.com/academy/keyboard-short cuts-revive-economy/.

145   study by the University of California, Irvine: Gloria Mark, Daniela Gudith, and Ulrich Klocke, "The Cost of Interrupted Work: More Speed and Stress," *CHI '08: Proceedings of the SIGCHI Conference on Human Factors in Computing Systems*, April 2008, 107–10.

147   twenty-second rule: Shawn Achor, *The Happiness Advantage* (New York: Crown Business, 2010), Part Two, Principle #6.

152   Data from the software company HubSpot: "Email Marketing: Open Rate Increased by Over a Quarter Compared to March," Netimperative, May 13, 2020, https://www.netimperative.com/2020/05/13/email-market ing-open-rate-increased-by-over-a-quarter-compared-to-march/.

153   around eleven times per hour: Gloria Mark, Shamsi T. Iqbal, Mary Czerwinski, Paul Johns, Akane Sano, and Yuliya Lutchyn, "Email Duration, Batching and Self-interruption: Patterns of Email Use on Productivity and Stress," paper, CHI Conference, May 2016.

163   One study by IBM: Steve Whittaker, Tara Matthews, Julian Cerruti, Hernan Badenes, and John Tang, "Am I Wasting My Time Organizing Email? A Study of Email Refinding," *CHI '11: Proceedings of the SIGCHI Conference on Human Factors in Computing Systems*, 2011, 3449–58.

169   A 2006 Duke University study: David T. Neal, Wendy Wood, and Jeffrey M. Quinn, "Habits—A Repeat Performance," *Current Directions in Psychological Science* 15, no. 4 (August 2006): 198–202.

171   Results of a study published in the *European Journal*: Philippa Lally, Cornelia H. M. van Jaarsveld, Henry W. W. Potts, and Jane Wardle, "How Are Habits Formed: Modelling Habit Formation in the Real

World," *European Journal of Social Psychology* 40, no. 6 (July 2009): 998–1009.

174   the power of temporal landmarks: Daniel H. Pink, *When* (New York: Riverhead Books, 2018), Part 2, chap. 3.

176   Kristen Fuller, MD, wrote: Kristen Fuller, MD, "JOMO: The Joy of Missing Out," *Happiness Is a State of Mind* (blog), *Psychology Today*, July 26, 2018, https://www.psychologytoday.com/us/blog/happiness-is-state-mind/201807/jomo-the-joy-missing-out.

188   regular meditation can: Matthew Thorpe and Rachael Ajmera, "12 Science-Based Benefits of Meditation," Healthline, May 11, 2023, https://www.healthline.com/nutrition/12-benefits-of-meditation.

190   as little as six minutes: Andy Chiles, "Reading Can Help Reduce Stress, According to University of Sussex Research," *The Argus*, March 20, 2009, https://www.theargus.co.uk/news/4245076.reading-can-help-reduce-stress-according-to-university-of-sussex-research/.

INDEX

Note: page numbers in *italics* indicate figures.

tools
  artificial intelligence (AI), 142, 164
  customizing, 140–141
  and efficiency, 138–139
  personalizing, 141–142
  productivity practices, 144
  settings exploration, 139–140
  shortcuts, 142–144
Tracy, Brian, 29, 36
twenty-second rule for habit breaking, 147
Twohill, Lorraine, 39

University of California, Irvine, 145
uptime
  achieving, 193–196, *194*
  defined, x
  fueled by downtime, 82–87
  holistic nature of, xi
  as productivity, x
urgent matters, dealing with
  blocking time for, 9
  Eisenhower method, 9–11, *10*
  fix the system, 11–12
  as a top three priority, 12
Uzodike, Junnifa, 86

vision, xiii

When (Pink), 174
when:then routines
  creating, 170–173
  memory attachments with, 173–174
  natural starts for, 174–175
  productivity practices, 175
Wieth, Mareike, 51
workflows, List Funnel, 40–42, *41*
working from home
  creating consistency, 104
  hot spots, 100–101, *101*
  hybrid work, 91–98
  not spots, 102–103
  productivity practices, 105
  staying in the flow, 104–105

"yes," saying
  as a "no" to something else, 19–20
  tactics for, 26–27
you-ser manual, 113–115

Zero-based Calendaring
  building blocks template, 58, 59
  example, 60–61, *61*
  implementing, 59–60
  as a practice, 54–55
  productivity practices, 62
  steps, 55–58
  unplanned days, 58–59

ABOUT THE AUTHOR

LAURA MAE MARTIN is the Executive Productivity Advisor at Google in the Office of the CEO. She coaches Google's top executives on the best ways to manage their time and energy and sends out a weekly productivity newsletter that reaches more than 50,000 employees. During her thirteen-year tenure at Google, she has worked in sales, product operations, event planning, and now executive coaching. Laura holds a bachelor of science in business administration from the University of North Carolina at Chapel Hill and lives in Charlotte, North Carolina, with her husband and three children.

More about Laura and resources from this book can be found at www.lauramaemartin.com.